Contents

DRUGS

A Parent's Guide

DRUGS 2009 REVISED FOR 2009

Need
- 2 -
Know

Judy Mackie

C153853282

First published in Great Britain in 2004 by
Need2Know
Remus House
Coltsfoot Drive
Peterborough
PE2 9JX
Telephone 01733 898103
Fax 01733 313524
www.need2knowbooks.co.uk

Revised Edition for 2009.

Need2Know is an imprint of Forward Press Ltd.
www.forwardpress.co.uk

SB ISBN 978-1-86144-043-3

Introduction

'Kids, 10, on coke as price plunges.'
'Heroin crisis is feared as kid is arrested.'
'Dance drugs wreck young lives.'
'Weekender drug deaths soar.'

Do these headlines look familiar? They should do – they're real-life examples of the sort that appear regularly in UK newspapers.

Not surprisingly, parents are frightened by such sensational stories, which are reinforced by TV and radio news reports, the storylines of popular soaps and the extreme experiences of chat show guests.

Surrounded by all this hype and horror, it's only natural to panic and wonder:

- How can I protect my child?
- How will I know he or she is taking drugs?
- What can I do to stop them sliding down the slippery slope towards dependency, bad health and serious social problems?

Well, the first step is to get a grip on reality. The myths surrounding drugs and drug use can be just as bizarre as any drug-induced hallucination – and are probably far more damaging to the way we live our lives and communicate with others.

Mistrust and misunderstandings based on these myths build barriers between generations and do nothing to address the real problems – both health-related and social – caused by drugs.

Yes, we live in a drug-taking society. Very few youngsters will not be exposed to drugs in some form or another. New drugs have appeared on the scene and children are experimenting at an earlier age. But all these facts should be kept in perspective.

'The myths surrounding drugs and drug use can be just as bizarre as any drug-induced hallucination – and are probably far more damaging to the way we live our lives and communicate with others.'

One of the biggest myths around is that use of highly-addictive drugs, such as heroin and crack cocaine, is rife among young people. In fact, according to the latest British Crime Survey (2007/08)*, within the youngest (16-24) age bracket, 0.2% had used heroin and 0.2% had used crack cocaine in the year prior to the survey being carried out. *This survey covers England & Wales.

Among under-16s, the latest regional surveys show that by far the most popular drugs are alcohol, cannabis and tobacco. Each of these carries its own risks, as we shall discover in later chapters, but they are far from being close to transforming an entire generation of young people into hopeless addicts with no future.

This book will help you, as a parent, separate the myths from the realities and form a clearer perception of the drug culture and why it is so attractive to young people. Together we'll look at different drugs and their effects, described first-hand by young users themselves; we'll discover what other parents and young people think about drugs; we'll consider the legal implications of drug use, and we'll find out how to seek professional support, if it should ever be necessary.

All this knowledge is very important because, as a parent, you have a crucial role to play in educating your children about drugs. You have the greatest understanding of and influence over your child's life. You know their likes, dislikes, needs, idiosyncrasies, fears and triumphs. National and local drugs education are undoubtedly useful, but when it comes to getting through to young people on an individual basis, you will know better than any teacher, counsellor or health worker what will make a real impact on your child.

Communication is the key to helping young people make the decisions that are right for themselves. And that doesn't mean delivering long lectures about drugs, or instigating the Spanish Inquisition every time they come home from a night out! Listening to your child, making time to chat regularly about what is happening in his or her life and generally building a good relationship with them will provide them with a strong and trustworthy base to return to when they need support and someone to talk things through with.

Most parents will argue that talking about talking to teenagers is far easier than putting it into practice. But good communication can be learned – and if it's not something you're confident about, this book will help you get started. Our practical guide will take you through the basic steps which you can use and develop to suit your own circumstances. Of course, these skills don't apply only to discussions about drugs. They will stand you in good stead in a variety of circumstances and will help you build better relationships within your family, based on trust and mutual respect.

One of the first steps to good communication is honesty. And when it comes to talking about drugs, that's where parents can fall down quite heavily. If you smoke and drink alcohol, you are liable to be called a hypocrite if you attempt to advise your child on the risks of taking drugs. Unlike older generations, young people see cigarettes and drink as drugs like any other, so think about and be prepared to be challenged on your own drug use.

Having climbed down from our pedestals, we're now in a better position to see the subject of drugs in a less sensational light. So forget the scare stories and stereotypes – here's the deal for real.

'Listening to your child, making time to chat regularly about what is happening in his or her life and generally building a good relationship with them will provide them with a strong and trustworthy base to return to when they need support and someone to talk things through with.'

Chapter One

Setting the Scene

One of the main reasons we as a society tend to panic about drugs is our collective fear of the unknown. The best horror filmmakers know the monster that's never revealed is far scarier than the one even the most sizzling Spielberg special effects can produce. And because many people still have little or no knowledge of illicit drugs and their effects, these have grown hideous in the public's imagination.

Up to the late 1980s, very little UK-wide statistical data had been gathered on drugs compared to information available on the use and effects of alcohol and tobacco. However, the situation has been steadily improving and a number of large-scale lifestyle surveys of young people have been established. The most recent of these – together with the latest available British Crime Survey and Scottish Crime Survey figures, which provide an insight into illicit drug use among 16 to 59-year-olds in England, Wales and Scotland respectively – can provide a broad picture of reported drug use today.

'One of the main reasons we as a society tend to panic about drugs is our collective fear of the unknown.'

Over-16s

The most significant finding revealed by the latest Crime Surveys is that drug use generally has steadily decreased since the mid-1990s.

According to the British Crime Survey (England & Wales) 2007/2008:

- 9.3% of 16-59-year-olds said they had used an illicit drug within the last year; the percentage was 11.2% in 1996.

Of those in the 16-24 age range:

- Use of any illicit drug in the last year fell from 29.7% in 1996 to 21.3% in 2007/08 (attributed to a gradual decline in cannabis use).

- Frequent use of any drug (defined as using any illicit drug more than once a month in the last year) decreased from 11.6% in 2002/03 to 7.3% in 2007/08.

- Cannabis remains the drug most likely to be used by young people: 17.9% used cannabis in the last year.

- 6.8% said they had used a Class A drug (see chapter 7) in the last year. This reflects a general decrease since 1996. Over the same period there were increases in cocaine use and decreases in the use of ecstasy and hallucinogens.

The Scottish Crime and Victimisation Survey (2006) reported:

- Although levels of lifetime drug use in Scotland were broadly similar to those reported in England and Wales in 2005/06 by the British Crime Survey, levels of current drug use were higher in Scotland compared with England and Wales.

- 13% of 16-59-year-olds reported taking one or more illicit drugs in the year preceding the survey.

- 31.0% of 16-24-year-olds had taken any illicit drugs in the past year.

- Current drug use in both the last year and the last month was highest among 16-19-year-olds and declined steadily with age.

- Cannabis was by far the most commonly used drug. 11% of all respondents had used cannabis in the last year. Cocaine and ecstasy were the second most commonly used drugs, having been taken by 4% and 3% of all respondents in the last year. Only 0.5% had used heroin in the last year and 0.4% had used crack cocaine.

Under-16s

But what about the reported drug use of young people under 16? Research has shown that during the period 1987-1995 there was a sharp increase in the number of 11-15-year-olds who reported taking illicit drugs in the UK. Figures rose less dramatically in the second half of the 1990s, stabilised between 2000 and 2003 and had decreased by 2006/07.

Let's look at some of these figures in more detail.

In England*

- In 2003, 21% of pupils aged 11-15 said they had taken illicit drugs within the last year. By 2007, the percentage had dropped to 17%.

- 12% of pupils had taken drugs in the last month in 2003. In 2007, 10% had taken drugs in the last month.

- In 2003, cannabis use in the last year was reported by 13% of 11-15-year-olds; this decreased to 9% in 2007.

- Among 11 and 12-year-olds, misuse of volatile substances was more common than taking cannabis; this was still the case in 2007.

- 42% of pupils had ever been offered one or more drugs in 2003; in 2007, this had fallen to 36%.

- In 2002, 10% of pupils said they were regular smokers; this reduced to 9% in 2003 and to 6% in 2007.

- 25% of pupils drank alcohol in the week prior to the 2003 survey; this reduced by 5% in 2007.

* 'Drug Use, Smoking and Drinking among Young People in England in 2007' – NHS Information Centre Survey by the National Centre for Social Research (NCSR) & the National Foundation for Educational Research (NFER).

In Scotland**

- In 2002, 33% of 15-year-olds and 11% of 13-year-olds reported that they had used drugs within the last year. By 2006, the numbers had reduced to 23% and 7%, respectively.

- In 2006, 10% of 15-year-olds and 4% of 13-year-olds said they had taken drugs only once; 8% of 15-year-olds and 2% of 13-year-olds said they had used drugs once a month, or more frequently.

- Cannabis was by far the most commonly used drug: 11% of 15-year-olds and 2% of 13-year-olds said they had used it in the month prior to the 2006 survey; this showed a substantial reduction since 2002, when the percentages were 21% and 6%, respectively.

- Use of drugs such as heroin and cocaine was very rare.

- In the 2006 survey, of the pupils who reported ever having drunk alcohol (57% of 13-year-olds and 84% of 15-year-olds), 14% of 13-year-olds and 36% of 15-year-olds reported having a drink in the last week. This had reduced from 20% and 43%, respectively, since 2004.

- Between 2004 and 2006 there was an increase in the proportion of pupils reporting they had never smoked: from 59% to 69% of 13-year-olds and 39% to 47% of 15-year-olds. In 2006, 55% of girls said they had never smoked, compared with 61% of boys.

** Scottish Schools Adolescent Lifestyle and Substance Use Survey 2006.

Summing Up

It's clear, then, the commonly-held perception that drug-taking is rife among young people and that they are turning to heroin and crack cocaine at a younger age is simply not borne out by the facts. Around 70% of youngsters under 16 are not using drugs at all and, of those who do use them, the main drugs of choice are alcohol, cannabis and tobacco.

But we should by no means be complacent about this. As we will see in chapter 3, each of these drugs carries risks for young people, whether these are short-term or long-term.

The issue of alcohol and under-16s is of particular concern to professionals involved in drugs education and treatment. According to UK voluntary agency Alcohol Concern, while the number of 11-15-year-olds who drink has dropped in recent years, the mean consumption of those who drink doubled from five units a week in the early 1990s to 10 units in 2004. Despite this, many parents do not take the issue seriously, some telling drugs workers quite openly that they would rather their child used alcohol than drugs. Considering that deaths in the UK as a direct result of alcohol almost doubled between 1991 and 1996 (a total of 8,758 deaths were directly linked to alcohol in 2006, compared to 4,144 deaths in 1991; note that these do not include accidents, violence and suicide as a result of alcohol) – and that alcohol accounts for four times as many deaths as do illicit drugs* – these parents are clearly not grasping the severity of the situation.

The same goes for smoking and young people, which again is tolerated by many parents as a 'less risky' alternative to illicit drugs. Yet, according to the latest estimates, each year around 114,000 people in the UK die from smoking-related diseases.

So to put things in perspective, the substances that are the biggest killers – alcohol and tobacco – are tolerated by our society far more than other drugs. But they are drugs just the same. Please bear this in mind as you read the rest of this book.

Now that we have a general idea of the UK drugs scene today, it's time to tackle some of the biggest obstacles to achieving a better understanding of drugs – the myths.

*A June 2003 report by the UK voluntary agency Alcohol Concern revealed that while 1,498 deaths in 2001 were directly related to drugs, nearly 6,000 deaths in the same year were a direct result of drinking too much alcohol (N.B. this figure does not include deaths caused by accidents, violence or suicide where alcohol is the contributing factor).

Chapter Two

Drugs - The Myths

Before we take a look at individual drugs and their effects, let's get a few things straight. Have your mallets at the ready, because here is where some of the most commonly-believed myths about drugs get a good bashing...

I know nothing

'I don't know anything about drugs.'

Oh yes you do! You may never have touched an illegal drug, but the chances are you have tried smoking or drunk alcohol at some stage, and perhaps still do. A lot can be learned from your own use of alcohol or tobacco – or prescribed drugs, such as sleeping tablets or anti-depressants, for that matter. If you think about it carefully, you may find that this use falls into some sort of pattern, becoming more pronounced during certain times of your life. Your reasons for choosing to use legal drugs may be similar to those which prompt young people to use illegal drugs. So the gap between you isn't as wide as you think.

- Be honest about your own 'drug career'. Remember your own teenage years – did you pay any attention to your parents' attitudes to going out, drinking, etc? If so, how did they get through to you? If not, were they too heavy-handed? Bear all this in mind when trying to communicate with your child about drugs.

> 'Your reasons for choosing to use legal drugs may be similar to those which prompt young people to use illegal drugs.'

Dangerous assumptions

'All drugs are dangerous.'

Thankfully, this is not the case, otherwise hospitals could not cope with the number of people needing urgent attention. Although there are certain risks attached to every drug – legal or illegal – most people who use drugs will come to little or no physical harm. More about risks in chapter 3.

'Illegal drugs are more dangerous than cigarettes and alcohol.'

In the UK, alcohol and tobacco account for far more deaths than illegal drugs do; remember, 8,758 deaths in the UK were directly linked to alcohol in 2006, while smoking kills around 114,000 people annually.

'One try of hard drugs, such as heroin or cocaine, is enough to get you hooked.'

Although it is easier to become dependent on heroin and cocaine than on other drugs, it takes time to develop a dependency. As with trying alcohol or smoking for the first time, trying drugs doesn't mean instant addiction. Even when dependent – either psychologically, physically or both – most drug users do eventually give up or control their use. More about dependency in chapter 3.

'Cannabis is addictive.'

You can't become physically dependent on cannabis, although some people become dependent on it psychologically i.e. to help them cope with everyday life. For more information about this drug and its effects, see chapter 3.

'Cannabis is harmless.'

This is a widely-believed myth. Some people do become psychologically dependent on cannabis, and, if smoked, it can also damage the lungs. Driving under the influence of cannabis is as dangerous as drink-driving, and the legal implications of getting caught in possession of the drug could ruin a young person's career.

'Ecstasy kills.'

Tragically, some young people have died from taking just one ecstasy pill. The latest available records show that there were 250 ecstasy-related deaths in the UK between 1990 and 2004. Many of these have been as a result of dehydration through a combination of increased body temperature due both to the drug itself and to prolonged dancing in a hot atmosphere. Another cause of death has been drinking too much water, resulting in swelling of the brain. The message now given to young people who use ecstasy is to drink water – no more than a pint an hour – only if they are dancing (and therefore losing water through sweat).

To put the dangers of ecstasy in perspective, hundreds of thousands of the tablets are taken every week in the UK, with no dangerous effects. But it is important to know that there is growing evidence to suggest that ecstasy has long-term psychological effects. For more about ecstasy and its effects, see chapter 3.

'Soft drugs inevitably lead to hard drugs.'

'Although most heroin users will have tried cannabis at some stage, it is not the case that most cannabis users will go on to experiment with heroin.'

Although most heroin users will have tried cannabis at some stage, it is not the case that most cannabis users will go on to experiment with heroin.

- Try not to see drug issues in black and white. Being too judgmental from the start will not encourage a two-way discussion with your child.

Don't tell me about young people

'Young people take drugs because they are bored.'

It's not as clear-cut as that. There are plenty of young people who have full and active lives, who also experiment with drugs.

'They're put under pressure to try drugs by their friends.'

The urge to be the same as their friends may encourage some young people to try drugs, but they still usually do it through choice rather than pressure. Teenagers who choose not to take drugs or alcohol are more often respected rather than ridiculed by their peers.

- Give your child credit for thinking for him/herself. Blaming their friends will only alienate them from you. Encourage them to bring friends home so that you get to know them as people – not rivals for your child's affection. That way, you'll be able to judge whether or not they really are a 'bad influence'. What's more important is that knowing about your child's friends gives you something in common and helps strengthen your relationship.

Us and them

'Drug-taking happens only in deprived areas.'

Not true. There is clear evidence that drugs are used throughout society by people of all backgrounds and classes.

'Drug dealers hang around schools trying to get children hooked.'

There are plenty of drug dealers around, but most have little or nothing to do with younger people because youngsters don't have that much money. Most young people tend to get their drugs from friends, older siblings and small-time users, rather than from strangers at the school gates. And it's worth remembering that many young people seek out drugs rather than having them pushed on them.

'If youngsters take drugs, their parents must be to blame.'

As we've seen, young people of all ages, classes and backgrounds take drugs for all sorts of reasons – positive and negative. Most of them choose to do so of their own free will – their upbringing has nothing to do with it.

'Normal youngsters don't take drugs.'

If you mean that only young people with serious problems take drugs, that's not true either. Drug use need not necessarily signify an inability to cope – it is also regarded as recreational by many young people; something that's fun and makes them feel good.

Drugs are used in all walks of life – and they're used for a variety of reasons.

Paying the price

'Most drug users turn to crime to finance their habit.'

Drug users who turn to crime tend to be dependent on heroin, crack or cocaine – drugs which are not popular among young people. Most young drug users are not dependent and can afford to buy drugs without having to steal to pay for them.

'But surely drugs are very expensive?'

Not those commonly used by young people. Drug prices do vary from region to region, but as a general guide, as little as £3 will buy a bottle of 'poppers' or a tab of LSD, £8-£12 will buy a 'wrap' of amphetamine, £15-£20 will buy a quarter of an ounce of cannabis and a tablet of ecstasy may cost £2-£5. Magic mushrooms grow wild in September/October, and solvents are cheap and freely available in shops and in the home.

- It pays to stay streetwise about the realities of drug-taking. Knowing the facts and figures will give you better credibility with your child.

It's good to talk

'We need to be stricter with our kids.'

Being too strict can have the opposite effect.

'The "Just Say No" message doesn't work, so there's no point in using it.'

This message may not work with some young people, but it does have an influence over the majority. Drug workers maintain that it is still important to use the simple message 'Say no to drugs' with children from an early age.

'"Drugs Kill" scare tactics put youngsters off trying drugs.'

Research has shown that scare tactics don't work. When young people discover drugs are not the instantaneous killers they are made out to be, they don't trust anything we say and may then start to believe that drugs are harmless. They, like all of us, need to be told the truth about drugs so that they can make informed decisions.

'That's right – once they know the facts, they won't experiment with drugs.'

If it were only that simple! While knowing the facts about drugs may make them more careful, it won't necessarily stop them using drugs. As adults, we know the risks associated with smoking and drinking, but that doesn't necessarily stop us using tobacco and alcohol. But knowledge is empowering, and young people who are well-informed about drugs are less likely to come to serious harm.

'Discussing drugs with children might encourage them to try them.'

This is not true. If you don't talk to your child about drugs, you can be sure that they will find out about them anyway. Isn't it better for them to hear the truth from you than half-truths from a less accurate source?

'But they're too young.'

Children think and hear about drugs from a very early age. It's never too early to start talking to them about drugs, as long as you do it in a way that's appropriate for their age. Don't rely on teachers to take sole responsibility for your child's drug education. Parents, more than any other adult, have an enormous influence over their children.

- If certain subjects have always been taboo in your family, you'll find it far harder to discuss them when you decide it's finally time to bring them into the open. But don't worry if you fall into this category – all is not lost. See chapter 6 for some basic communication tips.

Searching questions

'You can easily tell if your child is using drugs.'

Unless you see them high on drugs, it's almost impossible to tell. Think about it: many of the signs associated with drug-taking – such as mood swings, lack of appetite, tiredness and suspicious behaviour – can also be attributed to normal teenage life. In chapter 8, we'll cover these signs in greater depth, but these are by no means clear-cut evidence that drugs have been used.

'...many of the signs associated with drug taking – such as mood swings, lack of appetite, tiredness and suspicious behaviour – can also be attributed to normal teenage life.'

'If I knew what these drugs looked like, I might be able to tell if my child was using them.'

It's very unlikely that your child would leave drugs lying around for you to find. Another problem is that the same drugs come in different sizes, shapes and colours. Our guide to drugs in common use in chapter 3 will help you identify the most popular forms, but don't count on ever finding any – most young people use drugs outside the home. It's also important to remember that snooping around their bedroom will not help your relationship.

■ Rather than becoming obsessed with searching for signs of drug use, concentrate on building a trusting relationship with your child. That way, if there is any reason to suspect they're using drugs, you'll be in a far stronger position to talk to them about it and, if necessary, give them advice and guidance.

Summing Up

Well, did you recognise any of your own thoughts, fears and beliefs among these myths? It wouldn't be surprising, considering we are all exposed on a daily basis to misconceptions about drugs and what they do.

Now we've ditched the myths, it's time to look at drugs in a more rational, objective manner.

You might find what you're about to read in the next few chapters rather unsettling – perhaps even shocking – as we explore the realities of drugs and drug users. But it is far better to know and face up to what's actually happening than live in a fictitious world of terrifying tabloid headlines.

Chapter Three

What Are We Dealing With?

If all drugs were to be made legal and sold in the high street, their sheer variety of shapes, colours and associated paraphernalia would make a weird and fascinating shop window display, guaranteed to halt passers-by in their tracks.

In this chapter we're going to take a peek into the 'shop window' of drugs easily obtainable in the UK today. This may prove harder to do than it sounds: research has shown that many parents don't want to know the details about drugs – they think they know all they need to, which is that 'all drugs are dangerous'. But as you'll see below, that's a very simplistic view, which young people, particularly teenagers, will only scoff at.

It's far better to keep an open mind at this stage and find out exactly what we're dealing with.

First, though, let's look at the general risks associated with the use of drugs and alcohol:

- It is dangerous to mix drugs and alcohol.
- The user doesn't know for sure what is in the drug they buy.
- Loss of inhibition may lead to unsafe sex and unwanted pregnancy.
- Serious infections can be spread by sharing syringes.
- Accidents, arguments and fights are more likely after drinking and drug use.
- Heavy use can lead to mood changes, health problems and overdoses.

'...their sheer variety of shapes, colours and associated paraphernalia would make a weird and fascinating shop window display...'

Dangers

Drug use can never be 100% safe – but it is not always as dangerous as many people think. Professional drugs workers describe the dangers as depending very much on the three factors of drug, set and setting.

Drug

'The dangers of drug use depend on how much is taken, how often the drug is taken, other substances in the drugs, whether the drugs are mixed with other drugs and how a drug is taken.'

As you will see opposite, there are many kinds of different drugs and each has different risks and dangers associated with it. The dangers of drug use depend on how much is taken, how often the drug is taken, other substances in the drugs, whether the drugs are mixed with other drugs and how a drug is taken, i.e. whether it is snorted, inhaled, smoked, swallowed or injected.

Set

Personal factors involving the person using the drugs can be just as important as the drugs being used. These include whether the person is experimenting for the first time, their mood at the time, whether they have physical health problems, how tired they are, their body weight and whether they are male or female.

Setting

The place where drugs are used and what people are doing at the time can influence how dangerous the experience is.

The truth is, there is no simple answer to the question: how dangerous are drugs? But it's important that young people are aware that there are very real risks. And talking to them about drug, set and setting will be far more effective than telling them 'drugs kill'.

Classification

Time, now, for some window-shopping. Drugs can be classified as:

Stimulants

Stimulants (Uppers) are drugs which speed everything up, including thoughts, speech, physical movement and heart rate.

Depressants

Depressants (Downers) are drugs which slow everything down, including reactions, heart rate and breathing.

Hallucinogens

Hallucinogens alter a person's perception of reality, causing hallucinations and confusion.

A-Z of the most commonly used drugs in the UK

Here is an A-Z of the most commonly used drugs in the UK. You'll see that this includes alcohol and tobacco, which we have already discovered causes the most harm within our society. When you read how their effects and risks compare with those of the others, you'll perhaps understand why adults can appear hypocritical when warning young people about the dangers of taking drugs.

'...adults can appear hypocritical when warning young people about the dangers of taking drugs.'

2CB (hallucinogen)

Other names: bromo, nexus, CB, performax, spectrum, venus.
Legal status: Class A.
2CB (4-Bromo-2, 5-Dimethoxyphenethylamine) is a relative newcomer to the UK and is used in the dance scene as an alternative or complementary drug to ecstasy (to which it is chemically related).

Sold as white powder or small pills, the drug is normally swallowed, but can also be snorted or smoked. A standard dose (20mg) costs around £5.

The upside: depending on dosage, the effects of 2CB can range from increased energy and hallucinatory experiences to increased sensitivity to smells and tastes and sexual stimulation. When taken with ecstasy, it intensifies feelings of exhilaration and extends the duration of intoxication.

Duration: up to seven hours, from onset to 'coming down'.

The downside:

- Feelings of nausea and anxiety are likely to intensify if the drug is combined with ecstasy.
- 2CB should never be taken with anti-depressants.
- Regular use may leave the user feeling tired, anxious and disorientated.
- Other side-effects may include depression and, in vulnerable individuals, panic attacks and psychotic episodes.

'Drink makes me feel happy. It stops me feeling shy or nervous. I drink with my friends and we have a laugh.'
A 15-year-old girl.

Alcohol (depressant)

Other names: booze, drink, liquor.

Legal status: it is illegal to sell alcohol to young people under 18.

Alcohol is a depressant drug which slows down both physical and mental reactions. It has always been popular in the UK and is more commonly used today than ever before. It is widely available in supermarkets, off-licenses, licensed premises and most domestic homes. It is used by people of all ages for a variety of reasons, such as helping them to relax, have fun, forget their worries, lose their inhibitions and overcome fear or pain.

Alcohol ranges in price, but, for example, a beer-drinking man sticking to the government's safe ceiling of three to four units a day may spend upwards of £100 a week on his own alcohol consumption.

The upside: enjoyable effects include reduced inhibitions and increased sense of relaxation and wellbeing.

The downside:

- Alcohol use can cause aggressive and violent behaviour, serious accidents, unsafe sex, poor foetal development during pregnancy, death due to choking on vomit or an overdose caused by mixing alcohol with other drugs.
- Short-term use can lead to hangover, dehydration, headache, nausea and depression.
- Long-term heavy use leads to physical dependence and tolerance (the need

to take increasing amounts to achieve the same effects), and may damage the heart, liver, stomach and brain. It can also cause high blood pressure, problems with the nervous system and mental health problems.

- In 2006, there were 8,758 deaths directly related to alcohol. These did not include accidents, violence or suicide as a result of alcohol.

Amphetamine (stimulant)

Other names: speed, uppers.

Legal status: Class B (Class A if prepared for injection).

Amphetamine became notorious as a 'stay-awake' party drug used by Mods during the early 60s. There are many types of amphetamine, but the one most commonly used today is amphetamine sulphate.

The drug usually comes in the form of a white powder (but can be obtained in other coloured powder or tablet form), which can be snorted (sniffed), rubbed on the gums, dissolved in a drink or mixed with water and injected. Buyers are often short-changed by dealers who may cut the drug with other substances such as sugar or bicarbonate of soda. A wrap (small paper packet) of speed will cost around £8-£12 per gram.

The upside: enjoyable effects include sensations of alertness, confidence and well-being, raised levels of energy and stamina, and lessened desire to eat and sleep.

Duration: three to four hours.

The downside:

- Speed may cause psychological dependence and users may quickly develop a tolerance, resorting to increasingly larger doses.
- Short-term use may cause some users to feel anxious while using and tired and depressed afterwards. There is also a risk of sudden death from heart attack or stroke.
- Long-term use may result in disturbed sleep, uncomfortable itching, acute anxiety or paranoia, loss of appetite and aggressive behaviour.
- High blood pressure and calcium deficiency are also common among amphetamine users.
- Injecting the drug carries a number of risks – it may have been cut with other substances, which could damage the veins and internal organs. Sharing dirty needles may spread HIV and hepatitis, and injecting into an artery rather than a vein could cause gangrene.

'Speed makes my heart beat really quickly. It makes me go like a whippet. I can stay awake all night and the next day, no problem.'

A 13-year-old boy.

- For heavy users, the comedown can be unpleasant (although not physically dangerous) and may cause symptoms such as hunger, lethargy and depression.

Amyl and Butyl Nitrate (stimulant)

Other names: poppers; brand names: TNT, Liquid Gold.
Legal status: possession is not illegal but supply through sex shops and clubs can be an offence under the Medicines Act.

Amyl and Butyl Nitrate are vapours which, when inhaled, dilate the blood vessels and give an instant 'rush'. Available from clubs, bars and sex shops, they are used by people of all ages, often to enhance sexual pleasure. Poppers come in small flip-top plastic or metallic bottles costing between £3 and £5 each.

The upside: enjoyable effects include an instantaneous rush, caused by dilating blood vessels and a faster heartbeat.
Duration: around two to five minutes.
The downside:
- Short-term use can cause headaches, nausea and vomiting. If spilled, the liquid can burn the skin. It may be fatal if swallowed.
- Long-term regular use can lead to tolerance and an increase in the risks mentioned above.

Cannabis (hallucinogen)

Other names: dope, hash, blow, weed, grass, draw, zoot.
Legal status: Class B.

Cannabis is a mild hallucinogen and is by far the most popular illegal drug in the UK today. An extract of the hemp plant, which grows throughout the world, cannabis has been used recreationally in Europe for over a thousand years, but its properties for inducing sleep, stimulating appetite and relieving pain have been made use of in the East for many thousands of years.

In early 2004, all forms of cannabis (see below) were reclassified from Class B to Class C under the Misuse of Drugs Act (1971). This was reversed in January 2009. The debate is still ongoing as to whether or not the drug should be legalised.

'When you take poppers your head throbs and you think it's going to explode. Then it goes numb for a couple of minutes. You're supposed to keep poppers in your bedroom and if you're having sex, it's supposed to make you go faster.'

A 14-year-old girl.

Cannabis comes in three forms: marijuana (grass), the dried leaves and flowering tops of the female plant; cannabis resin, a brown substance scraped off the stem and pressed into a solid mass, and cannabis oil, which is refined from either the resin or the plant itself.

The drug's most active ingredient is a chemical known as THC. Different types of cannabis contain different levels of THC and, due to better cultivation methods, the THC content of today's cannabis is far higher than the amount found in the drug during the 1960s.

The most popular way of taking cannabis in all its forms is to smoke it, usually mixed with tobacco in a 'spliff' made from rolled up cigarette papers and a cardboard tip or roach. It can also be mixed with food and eaten.

Cannabis is grown illegally in the UK and is also imported from Holland, Central America, Africa and the Middle and Far East. Depending on its strength, it costs between £70 and £120 per ounce.

The upside: cannabis can be both relaxing and stimulating, making users feel sociable and happy. It also stimulates the appetite, and larger quantities or stronger strains may cause hallucinations.

Duration: the effects of one spliff may last two to three hours.

The downside:

- Cannabis is not known to be physically addictive, but psychological dependence – needing the drug to feel more at ease socially – can occur.
- Cannabis will often enhance the mood of the user and can therefore increase existing feelings of depression or anxiety.
- Because it reduces concentration and affects co-ordination, it should not be used when driving or operating machinery – and it is important to know that it can be detectable by some drug tests up to 30 days after use.
- Rare physical side-effects include rapid heartbeat, anxiety and paranoia.
- Research is showing that the drug can affect memory and the ability to learn new information.
- Users run a higher risk of having accidents while under the influence.
- The increasing strength of today's cannabis is giving rise to concern about its physical side-effects.
- A 2002 study by the British Lung Foundation found that three cannabis joints a day caused the same damage as 20 cigarettes.
- After heavy use, individuals may experience anxiety, irritability and sleeplessness.

'Cannabis gives me a good, drowsy feeling. I sit around and feel that I'm growing out of the ground. Sometimes if I've smoked a lot I see different colours and if I'm listening to music it sounds ace.'

A 13-year-old boy.

■ Long-term heavy use may lead to development or worsening of mental health problems.

Cocaine (stimulant)

Other names: coke, snow, charlie.

Legal status: Class A.

Cocaine, which is extracted from the leaf of the South American coca plant, has been used recreationally for centuries but was recognised as an addictive drug and banned from all but medical use in the US during the early 1900s. It became popular once again in the mid-1960s and is today widely available on the UK streets, although its high price makes it less popular with young people.

Cocaine most commonly comes in the form of cocaine hydrochloride – a white, crystalline powder, which, like speed, is often cut with other substances. The drug is usually snorted, but is sometimes injected. A gram of cocaine will cost anything from £40 to £70.

The upside: enjoyable effects include powerful sensations of alertness and confidence.

Duration: up to 30 minutes.

The downside:

■ Cocaine may cause psychological and possible physical dependence.
■ Blood pressure can be increased to the extent of causing a stroke.
■ Can cause convulsions and chest pain.
■ Too much sniffing can damage the lining of the nose.
■ Excessive doses can produce anxiety, sweating, dizziness, dry mouth, trembling hands and ringing ears.
■ Long-term use can irreversibly damage nerves and small blood vessels in the brain.
■ Heavy doses can cause aggression, frightening hallucinations and delusions.
■ 'Coming down' can be very unpleasant. Withdrawal may result in long-term depression.

'I've only ever done two lines and the only word I can use to describe coke is it makes you feel jellied... out of it.'

A 14-year-old boy.

Crack (stimulant)

Other names: rock, pebbles.

Legal status: Class A.

Crack, a very powerful form of cocaine which has been chemically separated from hydrochloride, first became available on US streets in the mid-1980s. It is gradually becoming more popular in Britain.

Crack comes in crystals or 'rocks', which are smoked in a pipe or heated on tin foil and inhaled. A small crystal costs £10-£20.

The upside: enjoyable effects have been described as being like 'a thousand simultaneous orgasms'.

Duration: around 10 minutes.

The downside:

- Crack may cause psychological and possible physical dependence. Users run the same risks associated with cocaine.
- The effects wear off rapidly, leaving users irritable, depressed and wanting to repeat the experience.
- Smoking crack is damaging to the lungs and may cause severe chest pains, bronchitis and asthma.
- Chronic use can cause severe damage to the heart and circulation, brain damage and severe mental health problems.
- Crack, together with methamphetamine, has been described by police as one of the worst drugs around due to its tendency to induce violent behaviour in users desperate for money to buy more.

Ecstasy (stimulant/hallucinogen)

Other names: E, mitsubishi, diamonds, euros.

Legal status: Class A.

Ecstasy (methylenedioxymeth-amphetamine, or MDMA) became popular in the UK during the late 1980s, with the advent of house music and the rave culture. Many young people now see the drug as an inextricable part of the dance scene, and it has been cleverly marketed as such. Song lyrics glorify E as an escape-valve to love and freedom, and the pulsating atmosphere of clubs and festivals where youngsters dance non-stop with their friends in a kaleidoscopic haze of shifting colours and light is conducive to the euphoric and energy-enhancing effects of the drug.

'I smoked it and got this instant rush, a fantastic high which made the hairs rise on the back of my neck. It was like taking speed, but far more powerful.'

An 18-year-old male.

In the UK, it is estimated that hundreds of thousands of people – and by no means all of them teenagers – regularly use ecstasy for recreational purposes. It is normally sold as a white, brown, pink or yellow tablet, or coloured capsule, fetching £2-£7 each.

The upside: enjoyable effects include rushes of exhilaration and euphoria; sensations are enhanced; inhibitions are lowered, and users may experience a warm feeling of universal love and friendship.

Duration: up to six hours.

The downside:

- Users may overheat and dehydrate without realising (see chapter 2).
- Very little is known about the long-term effects of ecstasy, although recent research is linking the drug to memory loss among long-term users.
- Ecstasy is not believed to cause physical dependence, but regular users do develop a tolerance and may become anxious, confused and subject to insomnia.
- Users can feel tired and depressed for a few days after use.
- May cause damage to liver, kidneys and brain, as well as mental health problems.
- As it acts as a stimulant on the metabolism, people with heart conditions, high blood pressure, epilepsy or any kind of mental illness should avoid using it.

GHB (depressant)

Other names: liquid E, liquid X, GBH.

Legal Status: Class C.

GHB (Gamma hydroxybutyrate) is a synthetic drug used as an anaesthetic. It appeared on the UK club scene around 1994. Although it is often sold as 'liquid ecstasy', it is not in fact related to ecstasy.

GHB normally comes as a colourless, odourless liquid (although it can also be found in capsule form) and is usually sold in 30ml bottles for up to £15.

The upside: 'Normal' (capful) doses may have the same effects as having a few drinks of alcohol. Causes euphoria, lowers inhibitions and increases libido.

Duration: can last up to a whole day.

The downside:

- When mixed badly, GHB can burn the mouth.

'When I take eccie it makes me think the music I'm listening to is the best I've ever heard in my life. If I've been arguing with someone, the anger suddenly goes away. It makes me so happy.'

A 14-year-old boy.

- Higher doses may cause sleepiness, nausea, vomiting, muscle stiffness and confusion. Very high doses can lead to convulsions, coma and respiratory collapse.
- GHB strength can vary from bottle to bottle, so it is hard to know how much is being taken.
- It is hard to tell the difference between a dose that gives a pleasant buzz and an overdose that could kill.
- Can be fatal when mixed with alcohol or other drugs.
- Users may lose consciousness.
- GHB has been linked to drug-assisted sexual assault ('date rape') after drinks have been spiked.
- The long-term effects are as yet unknown, but it's possible that tolerance, physical dependence and psychological dependence could result.

Heroin (depressant)

Other names: H, smack, junk, scag, gear, brown.
Legal status: Class A.

Heroin is derived from the opium poppy. Its close relative, opium, has been used by different societies throughout history. It was easily available in Britain during the 1800s and frequently used by rich and poor alike as an escape from pain, worry or drudgery, or simply as a pleasurable pastime.

Heroin is most commonly available as a light brown powder, which is injected, sniffed or smoked. Smoking heroin is known as 'chasing the dragon'; this involves heating the powder on tin foil and inhaling the fumes through a tube of rolled-up foil. Street heroin is frequently cut with other substances and sold in plastic bags or wraps. Heroin fetches between £10 and £20 per 0.15g bag.

The upside: enjoyable effects include sensations of warmth and wellbeing, all worries and pain melt away and it may induce sleep.

Duration: approximately eight hours.

The downside:

- Heroin users run a high risk of becoming physically and psychologically dependent on the drug, and tolerance (needing to take increasing amounts just to feel normal) is inevitable. However, this may take several weeks or months of heavy, regular use.
- First-time users often suffer nausea and vomiting as immediate side-effects.

'Heroin brings on a kind of euphoria… it makes me feel comfortable and warm and I feel good about myself. It sometimes helps me forget if there's something I'm upset about.'

An older drug user.

- The risk of overdose is high as the user cannot be sure of the amount of pure heroin in his or her wrap.
- For the same reason (as with any other injected drug), injecting can be extremely dangerous and may cause irreversible damage to veins and internal organs.
- Sharing needles carries the risk of HIV, hepatitis B and blood poisoning.
- Regular users may suffer from constipation and malnutrition. For women, the menstrual cycle may become irregular or may stop altogether.
- Withdrawal is not dangerous, but is extremely unpleasant, causing severe flu-like symptoms, cramps, nausea and profound mental distress. These symptoms are at their worst for two or three days and gradually fade over the next week or two. Heroin users say the worst problem with withdrawal is fighting their psychological dependence on the drug.

'Ketamine is a short-acting but powerful general anaesthetic which has been used for operating on humans and animals.'

Ketamine (hallucinogen)

Other names: green, K, special K, super K, vitamin K.
Legal status: Class C.
Ketamine is a short-acting but powerful general anaesthetic which has been used for operating on humans and animals. It comes as a white powder (sometimes in tablet form, sold as 'ecstasy') or as a liquid. It can be swallowed, inhaled or injected. Prices start from £25 per gram.
The upside: the drug has powerful hallucinogenic properties and can cause 'out of body' experiences. Effects depend on dosage, with low doses bringing on feelings of euphoria and rushes of energy, and higher doses causing similar effects to LSD (see over).
Duration: up to two hours.
The downside:
- Ketamine can affect different people in different ways.
- Can cause numbness and nausea, problems with vision, loss of co-ordination, temporary paralysis and frightening hallucinations that require assistance and reassurance from others.
- Because the drug causes users to feel no pain, they may hurt themselves without realising it.
- Ketamine is particularly dangerous if used in combination with depressants such as alcohol or heroin.
- Some mental health problems can be made worse.

- Tolerance develops quickly, requiring more of the drug to achieve the same repeated high.
- Prolonged use can cause psychological dependence, disorientation and detachment from reality.

LSD (Lysergic Acid Diethylamide) (hallucinogen)

Other names: acid, trips.
Legal status: Class A.

LSD was first manufactured in the USA during the 1940s as an experimental drug used by the CIA to rehabilitate victims of brainwashing and by psychiatrists to attempt to treat patients. The drug was popular during the 50s among musicians and writers who believed it enhanced their creativity, but its influence became widespread during the 60s when it reached Britain on a wave of psychedelia that changed the music and fashion industries forever, and opened a new and colourful perspective on the world for young people. Many music historians argue that without LSD, the psychedelic era would never have existed.

Acid comes in the form of illegally-manufactured 'tabs' – small squares of blotting paper printed with various transfer-style designs, such as strawberries, abstract shapes and cartoon characters. It can also come as tiny tablets called 'microdots' or 'dots'. Tabs and dots are dissolved on the tongue (it is a myth that LSD can be absorbed through the skin). Each dose costs between £1 and £5.

The upside: enjoyable effects – after half an hour or so, colours appear sharper, moving patterns can be seen and moving objects leave traces behind them. Later, amazing visions may appear; time seems to stand still and the user can think he/she is in an entirely different world.

Duration: may last up to 12 hours.

The downside:

- LSD does not cause either psychological or physical dependence and there is no evidence of long-term damage to the body, and little evidence of long-term damage to personality or behaviour. However, a bad LSD trip can cause nightmarish hallucinations and induce paranoia, terror and anxiety. It is not advisable to take the drug if you are feeling angry or upset.
- Trips cannot be controlled or stopped.
- It is possible that the drug could trigger psychotic behaviour in someone with diagnosed or latent mental illness.

'It takes about half an hour to have any effect and then your mind goes into a different place. I once thought I was being chased by Mars bars carrying knives and forks.'

A 14-year-old girl.

- It is important that the drug is taken in a safe place as hallucinations can distort judgement and may lead to serious accidents in areas where there are safety hazards.
- Unexpected 'flashbacks' (re-experiencing the effects of a trip) may also occur at a time when no LSD has been taken.

Liberty Cap Mushrooms (hallucinogen)

Other names: magic mushrooms, mushies.

Legal status: Class A when prepared for use (dried or stewed).

Magic mushrooms have grown wild in Britain for thousands of years, their hallucinogenic powers used to create mystical experiences during ancient religious rituals. They can be found in damp grassy areas between September and November and are used today as a natural (and cheap) alternative to LSD. The mushrooms, which contain the drug psilocybin, can be eaten raw, dried or cooked, and dried mushrooms are often made into a tea. Users will pick the mushrooms themselves or buy them dried for a few pounds.

The upside: enjoyable effects – between 20 and 30 mushrooms will create a powerful trip with sensations and hallucinations very similar to those produced by LSD, only milder.

Duration: around four hours.

The downside:
- The white Liberty Cap mushroom is similar to poisonous varieties. Dangerous mistakes can be made.
- The correct variety may still cause stomach pains, sickness and diarrhoea.
- May complicate existing mental health problems.

> 'I've picked and eaten mushies a few times. They're easy enough to find. They have the same effects as trips (LSD), but they don't last as long.'
>
> A 13-year-old boy.

Methadone (depressant)

Other names: meth, linctus.

Legal status: Class A if possessed without a prescription or supplied illegally.

Methadone is one of a number of synthetic opiates that are manufactured for medical use and have similar effects to heroin. It is used as a substitute for heroin in the treatment of dependency and, while it does not produce the same intensity of sensation as heroin, it is longer-acting.

Methadone comes in green, amber or blue liquid form, or as white tablets. The street cost is £1 per 10ml.

The upside: the drug promotes feelings of warmth, relaxation and detachment, and also may relieve anxiety.

Duration: effects can last several hours, depending on how much is taken and how often it is taken.

The downside:

- Like heroin, methadone is highly addictive.
- First-time users may be sick.
- Women can stop having regular periods (but can still conceive).
- Too much can cause coma or breathing to stop completely.
- Methadone should only be taken as part of a prescribed and supervised programme to treat opiate dependency.

Methamphetamine (stimulant)

Other names: crystal meth, christal, ice, meth, yaba, glass, chalk, crazy medicine.

Legal status: Class A.

Methamphetamine is a synthetic drug, closely related to amphetamine but produces stronger effects on the central nervous system. It comes either as a white powder that is smoked, injected, snorted or dissolved in a drink, or in tablet form.

Methamphetamine has been around as a medicine since 1887 and was banned from sale by UK pharmacies in 1968. Its street use and spread is of growing concern in a number of countries, including the USA, the Far East and Australia. It is still relatively uncommon in the UK, although its appearance on the dance scene here has led to fears that it will become more popular. The first convictions for illegal manufacture of the drug were made in the UK in December 2006.

The upside: even with small doses, users experience an instant rush of euphoria, wakefulness, increased physical activity, decreased appetite and, possibly, powerful hallucinations.

Duration: effects can last between four and 12 hours.

The downside:

- Common side-effects include nausea, panic attacks, compulsive repetitive behaviour and jaw-clenching.
- Users may experience paranoia and disturbing hallucinations, such as 'speed bugs', where they think bugs are crawling under their skin.

'The rush was immediate. I was filled with energy and felt like I could do anything.'

- Regular use is linked to lung and kidney disorders.
- Regular use can lead to dependency, with increased tolerance to the effects of the drug and physical and psychological withdrawal symptoms. Withdrawal can lead to severe depression and suicidal urges.
- Methamphetamine-induced psychosis can result in homicidal or suicidal thoughts and is also associated with violent and aggressive behaviour. Because of this it has been described by police as one of the worst drugs around.

Nicotine (stimulant/depressant)

Other names: cigarettes, cigars, fags, ciggies, smokes.

Legal status: it is illegal for retailers to sell tobacco to anyone under 16.

Nicotine, found in tobacco leaves, is a stimulant drug which increases pulse rate and blood pressure. Tobacco has been widely used in the UK since the early 1600s and smoking has followed numerous fashion trends ever since. During the 'age of innocence', before the full effects of tobacco were realised, cigarettes reached their peak of popularity in the 1940s when smoking was glamorised by Hollywood movie stars of both sexes. Today, smoking tends to be seen as a bad habit rather than an attraction – except, perhaps, by many young people (girls, especially) who still believe it enhances their image. On average, a pack of 20 cigarettes costs more than £5.

The upside: enjoyable effects – smoking helps regular users feel more relaxed and better able to concentrate.

Duration: the effects of one cigarette can last up to 30 minutes.

The downside:
- Chest and breathing problems are common among smokers.
- Smoking can restrict growth in young smokers.
- Long-term users run a greater risk of developing lung cancer, heart disease, circulatory problems, ulcers and premature ageing.
- Smoking during pregnancy can cause foetal damage.
- Passive smoking can damage the health of non-smokers and may cause babies and small children in particular to develop chest problems.
- Every year in the UK, more than 114,000 people die from smoking-related diseases.
- Withdrawal symptoms include restlessness, irritability and depression.

'If I smoke, I feel better – not so worried about things.'

A 16-year-old-girl.

PMA (hallucinogen/stimulant)

Other names: chicken yellow, chicken fever, mitsubishi turbo, killer.
Legal status: Class A.

PMA looks like – and is being sold as – ecstasy, but is much stronger. It is usually sold as white tablets which are swallowed. These cost between £3 and £8 each.

The upside: the enjoyable effects are very similar to those of ecstasy.

The downside:

- As little as a quarter of a tablet (60mg) is enough to significantly increase blood pressure, body temperature and pulse rates.
- PMA can cause muscle spasms and nausea.
- As the drug takes longer to take effect than ecstasy, there is a risk of users taking more, thinking it's not working.
- The risk of overheating is much greater than with ecstasy. If their temperature rises, users should seek help immediately.
- As with ecstasy, drinking too much fluid after taking PMA can be dangerous or even fatal. Users are advised to drink no more than a pint of non-alcoholic fluid per hour.
- PMA purity is suspect.
- Frequent use can cause paranoia and depression.
- Anyone with a heart condition, blood pressure problems, epilepsy or asthma can have a dangerous reaction to the drug.
- PMA is not believed to be addictive, but it is possible to build up a tolerance.
- The long-term effects are likely to be similar to those of ecstasy.

> 'PMA looks like – and is being sold as – ecstacy, but is much stronger.'

Solvents (depressants)

Other names: gas, glue, aerosols, correction fluid, marker pens, petrol, lighter fuel.
Legal status: it is illegal for retailers to sell butane gas refills to anyone under 18 and for solvents to be supplied to people of any age in the knowledge that they are to be misused.

Solvents are most commonly used by young people and are regarded by many health experts as being among the most dangerous types of drugs, as they can cause serious illness – even death – the very first time they are used. Solvents are usually sniffed (or 'huffed') through cloth or from plastic bags; gas may also be squirted straight into the back of the throat.

Users can be categorised as: experimental sniffers (try once or twice and then stop); regular sniffers (who go through a phase lasting several months and then stop), and long-term users (young people who tend to have problems in their lives and find solvents help them to cope).

The upside: enjoyable effects can be similar to those produced by alcohol. Solvents also cause an instant euphoric rush and may induce hallucinations.

Duration: from a few minutes to 30 minutes.

The downside:

- Between 70 and 100 deaths per year occur as a direct result of using solvents.
- Sniffing can cause heart failure. Spraying aerosols or gas into the mouth can freeze the throat and cause suffocation.
- Users also run the risk of suffocating if they are sniffing from plastic bags.
- Intoxication can cause some youngsters to do dangerous things.
- Short-term effects include a hangover lasting a day or two, nausea, vomiting, blackouts, bad cough, spots/sores around the mouth, persistent colds and heart problems.
- Long-term effects can be damaging to the brain, liver, kidneys, lungs, nervous system and reproductive organs.

'Glue is for glue-pots... nutters. I've taken gas a few times though. It makes me feel like a zombie. One time a Ninja turtle came and spoke to me.'

A 13-year-old boy.

Tranquillisers and Sedatives (depressants)

Brand names: Valium, Librium, Mogadon.

Other names: tranx, eggs, jellies, benzos.

Legal status: Class C (if possessed without prescription or supplied illegally). Tranquillisers and sedatives come in many varieties and are prescribed to alleviate anxiety and insomnia. These are meant to be used only for a few weeks as a coping mechanism during a crisis, but in fact there are hundreds of thousands of people in the UK who have regular, legal prescriptions – many stretching over periods of several years.

Tranquillisers most commonly used for recreational purposes (mainly to counteract the effects of stimulants) are benzodiazepenes such as diazepam (Valium), chlordiazepoxide (Librium) and temazepam, which, in gelatine capsule form, was withdrawn in Britain during the mid-1990s due to the risks associated with injecting it. These drugs are commonly found in medicine cabinets in pill or capsule form and are available on the street for around £2 per tablet.

The upside: enjoyable effects – in the short-term, these drugs will have a calming effect and aid sleep.
Duration: several hours.
The downside:

- Regular use for more than a few months can result in dependency, depression and aggressive and unpredictable behaviour.
- Mixing these drugs with alcohol is particularly dangerous and can result in overdose and death.
- Injecting temazepam from dissolved 'jelly' capsules is particularly dangerous as the substance can re-solidify in the body and cause serious problems such as abscesses, thrombosis and gangrene. As with all injected drugs, the risks of serious infection from needles also apply.
- Withdrawal causes unpleasant symptoms such as anxiety, panic attacks, irritability and insomnia. Long-term users who want to stop are advised to go through a planned withdrawal programme.

Mixing drugs

Some drug users may use a range of drugs to enhance or counteract effects. For example, someone taking a stimulant such as ecstasy or speed may later take a tranquilliser or smoke some cannabis to bring them down so that they can sleep. Dealers will often sell 'party bags' of mixed drugs for this purpose.

However, there is no accurate way to predict how a combination of drugs will affect any individual and dangerous reactions can occur between drugs, even those considered relatively safe in isolation. Alcohol, for example, can amplify the effects of other drugs, particularly tranquillisers and opiates, and can induce nausea and vomiting with cannabis and ecstasy.

Using barbiturates or opiates to come down from a high is also risky in that these are far more addictive than the ecstasy or amphetamine that is used in the first place. The best advice is not to mix any drugs – and that includes alcohol and prescription drugs.

'I get my jellies in 10s or 20s – that's how the dealers sell them. No way would I inject – I swallow them. Jellies make you feel weird. It's a bit like smoking hash – you just sit there and can't move or do a thing.'
A 14-year-old boy.

Summing Up

Well done! You've faced your demons head-on and you've found out that different drugs have different effects and risks associated with them. You've also discovered the sobering facts about alcohol and smoking, and how they compare with illicit drugs. It's likely you've made many interesting discoveries, which you'll want to think about and discuss with others – including, hopefully, your child.

Most people when they read about drugs find themselves fascinated by the subject – so is it any wonder that certain youngsters should want to try them out for themselves? Let's meet some of these young people and find out why they have chosen to experiment with different types of illicit drugs.

Chapter Four

Doing Drugs

Having looked at all the different types of drugs and discovered the risks attached, you might wonder why young people take drugs in the first place. As we saw in chapter 2, the answer to this is by no means straightforward.

Just think about why we all use drugs in one form or another. Why do we persist in smoking, drinking coffee, tea or alcohol and using painkillers and prescribed drugs when we know some of these may carry risks to our health and/or social life? There are a whole variety of reasons:

- To help control stress, anxiety, nervousness, loneliness or pain.

- To help us relax.

- To fill in time.

- To be sociable and socially acceptable.

- Because it's part of our culture.

- To give us a buzz.

- To make life more interesting or exciting.

- To attract attention.

- To rebel.

- Because they are easily available.

- Because they make us feel good.

- Because we enjoy them.

Youngsters may take drugs for any or all of these reasons. They may be having problems at home or at school – or they may simply be curious to try something they see as different, forbidden or exciting.

Young drug users talking

It's all very well to theorise, but the best way of finding out is to ask the drug users themselves. In the next few pages, young people from different social backgrounds share their drug-taking experiences.

'I started taking drugs when I was 11 because all my mates were doing it and we were bored. I've taken hash, speed, jellies, gas, acid, mushies... but I would never take heroin. There are heaps of dealers at school. They get the drugs from their dealers further up the ladder.

'I probably like hash and speed the best. They make me feel ace. I've had bad trips before. One time, on acid, I didn't know where I was and it was scary... another time I took a few jellies and suddenly I was two miles away from where I'd been and I didn't know how I'd got there.

'I've been drunk as well, but it did my head in. I laid at the edge of the river and got soaked. When I got home, I fell over the bin and knocked myself unconscious. I'm not really worried about what drugs do to you, but when I get older I'm only going to smoke hash.' Gordon (13).

'I started smoking cannabis when I was 12. I don't think I was pressurised into doing it. A couple of friends did it and I just joined in – they didn't force me or anything. I still smoke and I enjoy it. It makes me feel relaxed and I believe it's far better for you than cigarettes or alcohol.

'I think it's rubbish that cannabis leads on to harder drugs – statistics show there are millions of people using cannabis, but only a tiny amount go on to take heroin. I've tried speed once or twice, but that's all, and I've no intention of taking anything else.' Ruth (16).

'I've taken lots of different kinds of drugs – poppers, gas, hash, trips, speed. Me and my mates do it for a laugh. I had a scare with speed, though. My mum had to take me to hospital one night after I'd taken it because I was hitting my head on the walls and wouldn't stop being sick. They took tests at the hospital and told my mum I'd been taking speed. She went mental. She said if I did it again I wasn't her kid. I've not taken it since, but I still do hash and trips.' Julie (14).

> 'I started taking drugs when I was 11 because all my mates were doing it and we were bored. I've taken hash, speed, jellies, gas, acid, mushies... but I would never take heroin.'
>
> Gordon (13).

'I don't take drugs now, but I did for a while... hash, speed and alcohol. I think I did it because there was nothing else to do except stay in and watch TV.' Simon (15).

'My real dad takes drugs – he grows cannabis plants in the lobby. My cousin takes drugs too. I've taken hash, speed, gas, poppers, E, trips... they're easy enough to get hold of at school. I read a magazine about E and the side-effects and it worried me a bit, but I can't remember what it said now. Nobody my age takes smack – it's bad news.

'My mum says she'll disown me if I take any more drugs, but I know she used to sniff glue when she was a Mod. I've found some good places to hide my speed – in the thick sole of my trainers. But you've got to be careful – I once stood in a puddle and all the speed dissolved.' Andy (14).

'I first started taking drugs when I was 13. I started with cannabis. I didn't want to take it, but my friends had some and I didn't want to look uncool in front of them. I smoked cannabis for about three years, until one day somebody offered me some speed, and it was the same story. It wasn't long before I was taking any and every drug that came along – ecstasy, acid, cocaine, crack and eventually heroin. I'm now on a methadone programme and have reduced to 20ml, with the intention of coming off it altogether.

'Each drug has different effects. I don't even like cannabis – it makes me feel anxious and paranoid, but for a long time I couldn't leave the house or even have a bath without smoking some first.

'Speed never did anything much for me, although I made on to my friends that I was feeling hyper, like them.

'Acid was my real drug of choice. It would give me the great rushing feeling that I got from taking ecstasy, but instead of lasting only a couple of hours, it went on for about 12 hours. Everything is different when you're on acid. People say things, but you know what they're saying has a deeper meaning. You spend hours staring at something like a pen or the carpet and you're fascinated because they're moving in waves and their colours change. Everything is funny and you laugh a lot, although some parts of the trip can be scary. But as long as you remember it's just the drug and that it'll wear off after a while, you can go with it.

'My mum says she'll disown me if I take any more drugs, but I know she used to sniff glue when she was a Mod.'
Andy (14).

'On cocaine and crack, you feel invincible. Your nose and body go numb and then you start feeling you can do anything. You're not scared of anyone or anything – it gives you unbelievable confidence.

'Crack gives you such a blast that it can make you physically sick – but somehow being sick is enjoyable. That can happen with ecstasy and heroin too. As soon as you've finished your first pipe, you're itching for the next one. I've seen myself scrabbling around on the carpet looking for leftover crack, I've been so desperate. I've never felt a worse feeling in my life than when the crack ran out. It was just as well it was too expensive to get into properly – where I live, a tiny rock costs £50.

'As soon as I started taking heroin, I realised I'd made a big mistake. After only a few days of taking it, I started feeling really bad and I realised I had a habit. I went to the doctor, but it was a long time before I could get on a methadone programme and so I had to use heroin while I was waiting. With heroin you only get the high for the first few weeks of use. After that you're just taking it to be able to get out of your bed. Methadone doesn't give me a high or anything – I take it just to feel normal.

'Of all the stuff I've taken, alcohol affects me far worse the next day than any drug has ever done.' Simon (24).

'I've been involved with drugs since I was 14. I started with alcohol and then went on to cannabis, amphetamines, ecstasy, cocaine, heroin and I'm now on methadone. I'm about to start reducing from 60ml because I want off it. I'm sick of it.

'The reason I got into drugs was not so much peer pressure as curiosity. I wanted to find out what they were like. The only drug I was ever reluctant to take at first was ecstasy because I'd heard it could give you hallucinations. I didn't want that because I'd stopped taking acid after having a very bad trip. It was a nightmare I'll never forget. I was at a party and had taken acid and magic mushrooms. Suddenly I felt claustrophobic and had to go outside, but when I stood on the threshold of the back door, outside looked dark and menacing, while inside was all light and happiness. But then, when I tried to go back inside, it started to get gloomy and scary in there too. Eventually I managed to leave and set off along the street, but the trees had taken on horrible gargoyle shapes and I felt as if I was in a horror film. That trip put me off acid for life.

> 'I started with alcohol and then went on to cannabis, amphetamines, ecstasy, cocaine, heroin and I'm now on methadone ... I want off it. I'm sick of it.'
>
> Tommy (33).

'Anyway, I ended up taking ecstasy because all my friends were taking it at the weekends and I felt the odd one out. Ecstasy puts you in a good, euphoric mood. You feel all lovey-dovey towards anyone you meet. Or you can feel jumpy and you start chewing your lips and can't wait to get on the dance floor. Some ecstasy is so strong, all you can do is sit back and listen to the music until the come-on is finished.

'Speed caused me a lot of problems because I couldn't switch off. I couldn't sleep or eat when I was on it. I hated it after a while and stopped taking it.

'Crack is a horrible, nasty drug, and it's very bad for you health wise. I'm glad I never got into it properly. You're up and down in 10 minutes, but the feeling it gives you is like an allover-body orgasm. I've seen good friends punching each other to get the pipe back only a couple of minutes after taking a blast. I've seen people go downhill very quickly after getting addicted to crack. One couple even had their baby taken away, but they're not worried because the crack is more important to them. It's a real shame.

'When I smoked heroin, it gave me a great sense of wellbeing. I felt as if I was wrapped in cotton wool and I'd drift off, although I'd be aware of what was going on around me. That's what they call "gouching". It feels really good at the time, but the more heroin you take, the more you need. When you wake up after taking it, your first thought is "where can I get some more?" It's like there's something inside your body that needs to be fed.

'What really gets me is the way people look down their noses at each other, although they are all taking drugs of one kind or another. Someone who drinks thinks they're above someone who smokes cannabis. A cocaine user sneers at people who use heroin. Someone who's fortunate enough to have got themselves stabilised on a methadone programme thinks heroin addicts are "dirty junkies". It's sheer hypocrisy. Actually, I'd far rather be an addict trying to give up drugs than an alcoholic trying to stop drinking. It's nothing to do with snobbery – I just think it must be so hard to give something up that is in your face wherever you go. Alcohol is advertised all over the place and people are forever offering you a drink. Drugs are not up there in lights, thank goodness.'
Tommy (33).

Summing Up

These stories, worrying though they may be, are not deliberately sensational. They simply reflect the realities of drug-taking today. For some of these young people, trying drugs is a phase they will grow out of. Others may carry on and lead perfectly normal lives, while others may find their drug-taking increasingly difficult to cope with as it begins to bring them serious health and social problems. Hopefully, if they do, they will find the strength to seek help, as our interviewees Simon and Tommy have done. The range of outcomes, like the range of reasons for taking drugs, will vary enormously.

'...drug-taking, for many young people, is a part of growing up. But this does not mean every youngster is doing it or that everyone who tries it will end up dependent on heroin.'

What is important here is to face up to the fact that drug-taking, for many young people, is part of growing up. But this does not mean every youngster is doing it or that everyone who tries it will end up dependent on heroin.

All of us will remember trying out various new experiences during our teens. Even if you didn't take illegal drugs, think of smoking, drinking, staying out all night, sex and fast driving... or any other coming-of-age activity that you didn't want your own parents to find out about.

It's a frightening thought for parents that their children are going to do similar, or more worrying, things. But there is simply no way adults can prevent young people from experimenting with life.

However, what we can do is help educate children about the realities of life by acknowledging the highs, pointing out the dangers and ensuring that they know they can always confide in us, no matter what happens.

So how can we best put this into practice? The two key words are education and communication – and we'll look at these in the next two chapters.

- Bear in mind that most of us rely on drugs in one form or another.
- Think about your own reasons for smoking, drinking alcohol, tea or coffee, taking tranquillisers or painkillers.
- Try to keep an open mind about why young people may use drugs.
- Consider using some of the young people's stories featured in this chapter when you talk to your child about drugs.

Chapter Five

Drugs Education

It's very tempting for parents who know little about the subject to leave drugs education to schools. But, as teachers and anyone else involved in education will tell you, parents are in fact the best educators of their children as they have the most influence from the very beginning of a child's life.

Education network

Education of any kind works best if it is delivered consistently throughout society, i.e. by nurseries, schools, colleges, universities, libraries, churches and other religious organisations, health authorities, toy and games manufacturers, community initiatives, charities, police, voluntary services and all forms of the media. Parents and other members of the family play a major part in this network, reinforcing (or redefining, since it's not a perfect world!) what children are learning from these influences and showing how it can relate specifically to them.

Drugs education, guided by the National Drug Strategies of Scotland, England, Wales and Northern Ireland, is working in the same way. A vast network of national and local agencies and organisations, including and in addition to those mentioned above, is steadily developing to spread accurate information about drugs and drugs issues, with the aim of reducing drug misuse and minimising harm caused by drugs. Many also provide support for drug users and their families – see chapter 8. And again, as a parent, your contribution to this is vital. By reading this book, you are taking the first step towards helping to educate your child about drugs. But there are many more ways in which you can become involved.

'By reading this book, you are taking the first step towards helping to educate your child about drugs. But there are many more ways in which you can become involved.'

What's happening?

The next step is to find out what is happening in your area. To help you, here's a brief roundup of the main organisations involved in delivering drugs education.

Drug Action Teams

Drug and Alcohol Action Teams (DATs) are multi-agency co-ordinating groups active throughout the UK. Their role is to deliver the National Drug Strategy at local level. DAT members typically include representatives from the NHS, local authorities (education, social services and housing), police, the prison and probation services, and the voluntary sector. Responsibilities include commissioning and co-ordinating services, monitoring and reporting on performance, and communicating plans, activities and performance to their stakeholder communities.

Schools

In accordance with National Drug Strategy guidelines, secondary schools throughout the UK have introduced comprehensive drug education programmes into the curriculum, mainly within the Personal, Social and Health Education (PSHE) framework. Drug education is also delivered (at an appropriate level) at primary school, as it is now understood that by the time they reach secondary school, many children already have some knowledge of drugs. Often this is gleaned from such sources as older brothers and sisters, and television programmes which may not be well-informed.

A variety of programmes have been developed, many of them in conjunction with other local agencies. For example, these may involve differing degrees of input from health promotion workers, police education liaison officers, drugs workers, former drug users and other young people specially trained to talk to their peers about drugs. They may also take the form of role-play workshops, debates, exhibitions and a variety of other creative projects.

But however they are implemented, all of these programmes share the common aims of improving young people's knowledge of drug facts, helping them understand the legal, social and health-related consequences of taking drugs, and helping to raise their self-esteem so that they can make informed (and hopefully healthy) choices when faced with situations involving drugs.

Many schools are now closely involving parents in their drug education programmes. Some are holding drug awareness evenings for parents, which, again, may include other agencies such as support groups, community police and health education agencies. Others, within the context of the curriculum, are encouraging youngsters to ask questions at home about drugs, for example a classroom lesson on household substances that are harmful can be followed up by children asking their parents about things kept in the medicine cabinet. In this way, drug messages such as the dangers of certain drugs, why they are taken, etc, can be reinforced by the parents in ways which are familiar and specific to each individual child.

Other school initiatives include short courses for parents on effective communication skills and helping children learn outside the school environment, as well as group discussions on drugs education and how parents can help.

The National Drug Strategy also requires all primary and secondary schools to have drug policies on how to deal with drug-taking or drug-dealing in school (see chapter 7). In many areas, local authorities and individual schools have chosen to develop their drug policies in consultation with pupils, staff, parents and governors.

All in all, schools are undoubtedly playing a pioneering role in drugs education – but to do this effectively they need the support of parents.

'...schools are undoubtedly playing a pioneering role in drugs education – but to do this effectively they need the support of parents.'

Colleges and universities

Further and higher education are helping to reinforce drugs messages through such initiatives as start-of-term health fairs, ongoing health information and advice, and student counselling support.

Community education

Drugs education is central to most community education programmes, and there are literally hundreds of projects in operation throughout the UK.

These involve community-led activities ranging from after-school clubs and outreach projects teaching drug users about harm minimisation, to diversionary outdoor activities, video-making workshops and courses in assertiveness and stress-handling.

Health authorities

Government health education bodies, NICE (formerly the Health Development Agency), NHS Health Scotland, the Wales Centre for Health and the Health Promotion Agency (Northern Ireland), provide a plethora of drugs information and advice for the general public, health professionals, drugs agencies, workplaces and anyone involved in education. These include publications, posters, videos, websites, promotional launches and high-profile media campaigns. Materials – many of them targeting parents – are widely available either directly from the organisations or from health centres, local health authorities, drug agencies and voluntary groups.

The individual health promotion divisions of local health authorities throughout the UK are also involved in a diverse range of drugs education activities. Working in partnership with schools, parents, private enterprise, police forces, local authorities and voluntary organisations, they provide young people and adults with consistent messages about drugs.

Police

Each police force has an active community education division, which involves dedicated police officers working in partnership with local health and education authorities and a range of other agencies to provide factual information that aims to reduce use of drugs, harm caused by drugs and crime associated with drugs.

Drugs services

A complex network of government, local authority and independent drug services exists throughout the UK, providing general drugs information and advice, as well as support for drug users and their families and friends. See details of national organisations (which can provide local contacts) at the back of this book.

Voluntary organisations

Again, there are hundreds of voluntary organisations providing information, support and advice relating to drugs. Some national contact details are available in the help list.

The Internet

Start surfing the Internet for drugs information and you could sit for days scrolling through hundreds of pages of material that ranges from the reliable to the downright disturbing. To make life simpler we've included a list of trustworthy websites in the help list, many of which are designed with young people in mind. As most of us are aware, the Internet is a double-edged sword: on the one hand it's an invaluable resource, supplying instant information on anything you care to think of. On the other, it is not at all discerning about what it provides, so if you or your child want the facts, it's best to consult the officially-recognised sites – and treat everything else as entertainment.

Start talking - and listening!

The very first piece of advice each one of these organisations will give to you as a parent is to start (or continue) communicating with your child about drugs. And to do this meaningfully you need to find out how much he or she already knows about them.

If this sounds daunting, don't worry. In the next chapter we'll look at how you can broach the subject and keep the lines of communication open. But first, let's see what youngsters and parents think about drugs education, and how they feel about talking to each other about drugs.

Young people

'I think drugs education needs to be more shocking. It's too factual and not scary enough.' Audrey.

'I'd like to hear more about people's experiences with drugs, rather than about the drugs themselves.' Calum.

'I learned about the dangers of taking drugs from a former heroin addict. That was enough to put me off taking them.' Alex.

'We should respect our parents' experience. They're not aliens – they've gone through adolescence themselves and we should be able to learn from them.' Anna.

'We probably know more about drugs than our parents do. Certainly, my mum doesn't have a clue. I think some parents are worried because they don't know or don't understand what's going on.' Samantha.

'Parents want to leave drugs the way they were when they were young. They don't like the idea of new drugs being on the market because they can't relate to them.' Philip.

'We need a society where the barriers are down and adults and kids can talk. Parents think drugs equal death and kids think drugs equal fun. Parents need to recognise the good side and kids need to recognise the bad side. A lot of people are taking drugs and having fun, and are not addicts.' Beverley.

'I think parents shelter themselves and their children from drugs.' Eric.

'I'd be scared to mention drugs to my parents in case they thought I was taking them.' Sue.

'If I was a parent, I'd want my child to think about how getting involved in drugs might affect their family and friends.' Rob.

'You need to learn about drugs at primary school because as soon as you get to secondary school, there are plenty of people who will ask if you want any.' Brian.

Parents

'As someone who works with young people who take drugs, I know how important it is to discuss drugs with your children from an early stage. As a parent, I understand how difficult it is to find the time or the opportunity to do this. But no matter how busy you are, you need to keep communicating with your youngster and showing that you're interested in what they're doing – and that doesn't apply just to drugs, but to all aspects of their lives.' Ewan.

'One of the main things I need to know is how to recognise the symptoms of drug use and what to do if I find my children are taking drugs.' Jonathon.

'I would love to be able to talk to my teenage kids about drugs, but they just won't have it. As soon as I start to broach the subject of drugs or sex, they just roll their eyes and say "you don't have a clue".

'They seem to know it all already, but what worries me is that I don't know what they're up to. They certainly wouldn't come and tell me if they were taking drugs. My daughter didn't even tell me when she started her periods! I was really hurt about that because I thought she'd want to share that with me, but she couldn't see why I was so upset.

'I like to think I'm a good listener and I'd love us to communicate more, but they're just not the kind of kids who like to sit around and discuss things.' Rita.

'I've always tried to act on my belief that I should trust and respect my son as an equal human being, and not try to control him or keep things from him. It's not always easy – lots of times you want to tell kids what to do or what to think, or just tell them to shut up and leave you in peace!

'My son knows I love him and that we can speak about anything at all. I'm under no illusions that he'll want to experiment with drugs when he's older and I have to respect that. I trust him to make the right decisions, but if he gets in any trouble, he knows he can come to me.' Lindsay.

Summing Up

Drugs education is going on all around us. The main message coming through for parents is to start talking to their children about drugs – and the earlier, the better. But many parents find it hard to communicate with their children at all, especially if they are going through adolescence. As one parent puts it: 'How do you start a meaningful conversation with someone who scowls at you if you so much as ask them to pass the salt?'

It would be all very well to say that if you had put good parenting and communication skills into practice at an early stage, you would already have a strong enough relationship with your child so that he or she would feel happy to share their innermost secrets with you while growing up.

'How do you start a meaningful conversation with someone who scowls at you if you so much as ask them to pass the salt?'

But this is the real world and there is no such thing as the perfect parent. You may now regret not investing enough time in communicating with your child in the past – but that is in the past. Let it go. Remember that there are many positive steps you can take to improve your relationship in the present and future, and the next chapter will help you make a start.

Alternatively, you may feel that you have built up a close, trusting relationship with your child over the years, but that it doesn't seem to be helping at this stage in their lives. It's natural to feel disappointed and let down if you feel they are rejecting years of love, trust and friendship by no longer sharing details of their lives. But it's also natural for young people to withdraw from their parents while they build their own world, with friends taking centre stage.

In each case, the most important thing you can do is try to keep talking to each other.

- Always remember that you as a parent have an enormous influence in educating your child.

- Make an effort to find out what kind of drugs education initiatives are happening in your area and where you can get more information and support if you need it.

- Use the Internet wisely – and teach your children to do the same.

- Ask your child's school how you can help continue their drugs education at home.

Chapter Six

Keep Talking - Practical Communication Skills

Most of us are probably aware that good communication helps to build close, trusting relationships and that poor communication can lead to misunderstandings and alienation from others. But how many of us are good at putting good communication into practice?

In this chapter we concentrate on face-to-face communication, looking at ways in which we can improve our own skills and at the same time encourage others – not just children and teenagers – to respond positively to our efforts. These skills are valuable tools which can be applied in any situation where good communication is important, for instance when talking meaningfully to our partners, family, friends or colleagues.

So what is 'good communication'?

Good face-to-face communication is as much about listening and observing as it is about talking.

Think of someone you know who likes to talk, but not to listen. How do you feel when you try to tell them something and they dismiss it either by changing the subject or by 'hi-jacking' the topic and relating it to their own experience?

It's very likely that you feel rejected. You realise that this is not a two-way conversation at all and that you're being used simply as a sounding board by a selfish person who probably knows little or nothing about you. It's not a pleasant experience.

But if we're really honest with ourselves, aren't we all a little guilty of not listening at times?

There are many distractions in our lives which prevent us from taking time to really listen to what even those closest to us are trying to tell us. We talk at each other across a cacophony of white noise produced by the television, radio, computer games and CD players which dominate our leisure time at home; we exchange hurried messages in the short periods before dashing to work, or over a quick meal before rushing away to evening classes/sports events/pubs and clubs. We are slowly losing the art of really talking and listening to each other.

The good news is that we can do something about it – starting today. Before we tackle talking, let's take a look at the two other closely-related components of good communication – listening and observing.

Listening and observing

In good communication there should be far more to listening than simply hearing what is being said. We need to understand – and to understand not only what someone is telling us, but also why they are telling us and if they are telling us what they truly believe. In other words, we need to know where they're coming from.

Life would be far simpler if we all said what we meant. But we don't. There are all kinds of reasons for this, but two of the most important are that we don't want to be vulnerable and we don't want to hurt those we love. And so, afraid to expose our true feelings, we underplay our emotions, tell half-truths, lie outright, keep our thoughts to ourselves, say the opposite of what we mean... the list is endless!

It's best, then, not always to take what you hear at face value unless you are sure the speaker truly believes what he or she is saying. But how can you tell? That's where observation comes in.

How many times have you wished during an important telephone conversation that you could see the speaker – that it would help you understand more clearly where they're coming from? In face-to-face conversation we have the advantage of observing body language.

Many hundreds of books have been written about body language over the years and it's still by no means a cut-and-dried subject. Current thinking suggests that if you're trying to understand what someone is really trying to tell you, there's little point in consulting a body language 'dictionary' of typical facial expressions and gestures. These tend to be very general and can be open to misinterpretation.

It's far more helpful for our purposes to remember that, assuming the person we are communicating with is not a stranger, we will know them enough to be able to tell in most cases how they feel about what they are saying. Think about it: you've seen your children or partner reacting to many thousands of different situations over the years – you, probably more than anyone else, will understand their idiosyncratic expressions and gestures. You know when they're feeling unwell, angry, happy, excited, sullen, hopeful and so on. All you need to do is pay attention, and, to quote an old song, 'listen with your eyes'.

Active listening

Active listening involves a degree of talking and is one of those skills that is easy enough to understand, but hard to put into practice! However, it is well worth persevering with as it is especially useful in the case of emotionally difficult conversations.

Basically, active listening helps an important conversation to progress and develop, and hopefully this will lead to mutual understanding. Without active listening, conversations can break down, become inane or degenerate into arguments, leaving both parties feeling dissatisfied and no further forward in understanding the other's point of view.

Active listening involves

- Setting your own feelings aside and really listening to what you are being told.

- Observing the speaker to see how he/she is feeling.

- Making an effort to understand where he/she is coming from.

- Showing you do understand and are sympathetic – by nodding, using appropriate facial expressions, etc.

- Not being judgmental.

- Not interrupting with solutions, arguments or indignant remarks.

- Thinking of yourself as a mirror, reflecting back what the other person appears to be feeling and trying to tell you.

Here is an example of how active listening can turn a potentially explosive exchange into a meaningful conversation.

Without active listening

Mother: 'Why aren't you going out tonight, Sheila?'

Teenage daughter (on the verge of tears)**:** 'Danny doesn't want to see me any more. He finished with me this afternoon.'

Mother: 'Never you mind. There are plenty more fish in the sea. I didn't like that boy anyway – he had no manners and he always seemed to look down on you...(door slams) Sheila! Where are you going?'

With active listening

Mother: 'Why aren't you going out tonight, Sheila?'

Teenage daughter (on the verge of tears)**:** 'Danny doesn't want to see me any more. He finished with me this afternoon.'

Mother: 'Oh, no... you're very upset. He means a lot to you, doesn't he?'

Daughter (sobbing)**:** 'I really love him, Mum. I thought he felt the same way. Now I feel he was just using me.'

Mother: 'It's okay to cry, pet. It's horrible to feel someone has used you. Will this make things awkward for you at school?...'

As we can see, active listening has helped this conversation progress from a three-second disaster to a longer discussion about how the girl will cope with being rejected by her boyfriend.

Although the mother feels furious with the boy for hurting her daughter, she knows her anger is not important here. What matters is how her daughter is feeling and how she will come to terms with what, at any age, is a traumatic situation.

Resisting the temptation to judge and give your opinion is extremely difficult. We all like to think we can solve other people's problems and can pontificate for hours about how things should be. But as our example above demonstrates, this is not helpful at all.

However, if you're asked for your opinion, be honest. Take our example above: if the woman's daughter were to ask her if she is angry with the boy, there would be no reason for the mother not to admit that she is indeed angry. But rather than rant on about his bad points, it would be far more beneficial to then ask her daughter if she feels angry too. That could lead to her daughter listing all his bad points and perhaps realising for herself that he is not worth all the upset. Human nature being what it is, if she hears herself say it, rather than her mother telling her, she is more inclined to believe it!

Hopefully, this conversation will have brought mother and daughter closer together and laid the foundations for other important discussions in the future.

Talking

As we've seen, good listening skills can help make talking easier. Active listening will usually prompt a response from which you in turn can take your cue. It may be slow, hard or even painful, but you will find that eventually you will reach a point where you are getting to the heart of the matter and are truly communicating with each other.

But all this begs the question that you're engaged in conversation in the first place. We've ignored what can often be the biggest stumbling block of all – getting started.

Initiating an important conversation may be nerve-wracking, awkward or embarrassing if you're not confident about how to go about it. Supposing the person you are addressing becomes scornful, hostile or defensive? What if it

'We all like to think we can solve other people's problems and can pontificate for hours about how things should be.'

develops into a full-scale row? 'Getting heavy' is often a daunting prospect and it's easy to see why we can all at times find better things to do than broach a difficult subject.

Getting started

As we've seen in chapter 5, the first step towards effective communication about drugs is to find out how much your child knows. This example suggests a way of broaching the subject of drugs in order to do this. It's by no means a formula that should be followed to the letter (if only it was that easy!). You may not believe it at the moment, but you are the one who knows best how to talk to your child. Just remember to listen, observe and respond in a way which encourages further conversation.

> 'You may not believe it at the moment, but you are the one who knows best how to talk to your child. Just remember to listen, observe and respond in a way which encourages further conversation.'

- First of all, choose your moment. This in itself is a tricky task as many families spend much of the time doing their own thing in separate rooms or outside the home. Try to pick a time when you are not tired or hungry. Perhaps this could be after the evening meal (during is not a good idea, as difficult or important conversations have a habit of causing indigestion!) or at a quiet time during the weekend.

- Involve other members of the family if you can – this is a subject to which everyone can contribute and it makes the conversation less formal and intimidating. Drugs can be discussed in many different contexts, and, unless you want to tackle a particular issue in private (e.g. if you have reason to believe your child is taking drugs and want to find out if this is true), broaching the subject during a normal family gathering can be beneficial for younger children and grandparents who may know very little about drugs.

- Introduce the subject as naturally as possible. You might want to use this book as a starting point, e.g.: 'I've been reading a book on drugs and I had no idea that magic mushrooms can be found all over the country/drugs are so easily available in schools/heroin is not so popular with young people as I'd thought,' etc. Whatever you say, it must be genuine – remember, your child knows you as well as you know him/her and the last thing you want them to think is 'oh-oh – here comes the Spanish Inquisition'.

- Observe the response. If it's sighs and rolling eyes, don't be put off. This could mean that they think you're out of your depth or they know more than you do, or they think they're in for a lecture. So surprise them – bow to their greater knowledge with, for example: 'Oh, it looks like you know all about drugs – you learn about them at school, don't you? Did you know, though, that...'. This challenge to their superior intellect will hopefully be too tempting to ignore and the conversation could then go down many interesting paths. If the reaction is positive and your child volunteers some information, don't be tempted to jump in with such emotive phrases as: 'promise me you'll never take drugs'/'your father would kill you if he found out you were taking drugs,' etc. Remember to practise active listening.

- If you're challenged about your own drug use, i.e. of painkillers, tranquillisers, alcohol or smoking, don't get defensive. Be honest about why you use them and acknowledge the damage these drugs are causing in our society. Again, this could lead into a lively discussion and it may enable you to broach the important issues of health and the law. If the conversation is going well and your child is responding positively, try passing on some of the information you have learned in this book (see chapters 3 and 7 for the health and legal implications of taking drugs). But be prepared to be challenged, as myths about drugs are just as common among young people as they are among adults. This is a good opportunity to hammer a few on the head!

- If you are feeling confident, steer the conversation in a more personal direction. Ask if your child/children know anyone who takes drugs. If they tell you they do, remember not to panic or be judgmental. Listen to what they are saying and try to understand how they are feeling and what they really think about their friends' drug-taking. Do they appear frightened/curious/ashamed/defensive/disgusted/admiring/tolerant? Use active listening to reflect that feeling back. For example, if the child appears to be frightened, why not say: 'You seem to be a bit worried about that. Are they trying to get you to take cannabis too?' Alternatively, if the child seems to admire his/her friend's behaviour, you could say: 'Do you think he's quite brave, then? Do you wish you could do it too?' Seeing that you are not angry or upset may encourage them to confide in you further.

- If the response is extreme embarrassment, hostility or defensiveness and you suspect your child is not just being loyal to his/her friends, again, don't panic. Calmly say: 'This conversation seems to be upsetting you. Is there something worrying you?' This is a good time to let them know that if something is worrying them they can always count on you to be there for them. If they see you are not angry or judgmental this may encourage them to talk further, but even if they make it obvious that the conversation is over, they will not forget your caring attitude and will know they can broach the subject when they're ready.

- If it does come out that your child is using drugs, you will undoubtedly feel shocked, distressed and out of your depth. Chapter 8 will help you find the best way of coping with this situation, whether you choose to do this on your own, as a family or with the help of a support agency.

Summing Up

All these pointers to communicating effectively with your child may lead you in many directions. The first conversation could well pave the way for regular discussions which could turn out to be enjoyable experiences for the whole family.

For the purposes of this book, the subject here has been drugs. But it can't be stressed enough that these techniques could equally apply to discussing any topic under the sun.

Good communication takes practice and patience. It also comes with a degree of responsibility. Once you have opened the door and shown that you can truly listen and understand, you can't just slam it shut when it suits you. You may not always be in the mood to talk when your children/partner want to discuss something, but it's worth making the effort to give them the time they are asking for.

Building a trusting, loving, communicative relationship is not easy – but it can bring wonderful rewards which will last a lifetime.

- Make sure you understand what good communication is all about.

- Know the benefits of listening and observation.

- Learn the basics of active listening.

- Use our 'Getting Started' guide to help you broach the subject of drugs with your child.

- Remember – these skills will stand you in good stead no matter who you are talking to.

'Building a trusting, loving, communicative relationship is not easy – but it can bring wonderful rewards which will last a lifetime.'

Chapter Seven

Drugs and the Law

18-year-old John landed a job as a driver for a pharmaceutical company. A keen motorist, he was delighted with the job and took pride in his work. A few months later, he was caught in possession of cannabis (only enough for his own use). His court case was covered in the local newspaper. Soon afterwards, his employer sacked him.

Mary is 16 and uses hallucinogenics. Following a number of visits from the police, her furious parents threw her out of the house. Mary is now a prostitute.

James (19) is studying languages at college. A year ago, he was convicted for supplying ecstasy. Recently, he has applied for a visa to travel abroad. He has been refused visas for two out of the three countries he wanted to visit.

Helen was expelled from her fee-paying school for sharing a joint of cannabis with two friends. This happened before she was due to sit her Higher Grades. Since then, she has been unable to find another centre in which to sit her exams and now she fears she has lost out on the possibility of further education.

During his teens, Jack had a number of convictions for possession of various drugs. Now 26, he has been drug and conviction free for eight years. He recently applied for a job which required candidates to declare any previous convictions. Unaware of the implications, he did not declare his. He was offered the job, subject to a check on previous convictions. A few days later, the offer was withdrawn.

As well as being aware of the various health issues connected with drug use, it's important that parents and their children are clear about the legal implications of being caught in possession of illicit substances. As we can see from the real-life cases above, these can be far more extensive than some youngsters may imagine.

'…it's important that parents and their children are clear about the legal implications of being caught in possession of illicit substances.'

The facts

Illegal drugs are categorised under the Misuse of Drugs Act (1971), as follows:

Class A drugs

Heroin, cocaine and crack, LSD, ecstasy, methadone (which has not been prescribed for you), magic mushrooms (if made into a preparation), amphetamines (if prepared for injection), methamphetamine or any Class B drug which is injected.

Penalties: up to seven years imprisonment and/or an unlimited fine for possession; life imprisonment and/or an unlimited fine for supplying or production.

Class B drugs

Cannabis*, amphetamines (if not injected), barbiturates, Ritalin and Codeine.

Penalties: up to five years imprisonment and/or an unlimited fine for possession; up to 14 years imprisonment and/or an unlimited fine for supplying or production.

*Cannabis was reclassified from a Class B to a Class C drug in early 2004. This was reversed in January 2009.

Class C drugs

Ketamine, GHB, minor tranquillisers, anabolic steroids.

Penalties: up to two years imprisonment and/or an unlimited fine for possession; up to 14 years imprisonment and/or an unlimited fine for supplying or production.

Drugs which are not illegal

Solvents are not illegal and it is estimated that every household contains at least 30 sniffable products. It is illegal for shopkeepers to sell solvents to minors if they suspect the products will be used for sniffing, and it is also illegal for them to sell lighter fuel (butane) to under-18s whether or not they know it will be used for intoxicating purposes. In Scotland, sniffing solvents can mean young people under 16 can be referred to the Children's Panel.

Did you know it is an offence to...?

■ Be in possession of small amounts of a drug for your own use?

■ Be in possession of small amounts of a drug which you intend to sell or give to someone else?

■ Be in possession of large amounts of a drug which you intend to sell or give to someone else?

■ Send drugs abroad or have them sent to you?

■ Grow or manufacture drugs?

■ Allow someone to use your home to use or sell illegal drugs?

Parents should be particularly aware of the last two points, as they may find themselves being held responsible for their child's drug use in the home.

What is important to note here is...

■ If you find what you think is an illegal drug, you must either hand it to the police or destroy it.

■ The police can search your house without your permission if they have a warrant. If they do have your permission, they can search the house – including your child's room, with or without the youngster's consent – without a warrant.

■ The plant in your son/daughter's room which you suspect may be cannabis is illegal – and you could be prosecuted if it is discovered.

- Parents are not legally bound to tell the police if they know or suspect their children are taking or supplying illegal drugs.

The police can also stop and search anyone on the street if they have reasonable suspicion that the individual may be in possession of drugs.

School drug policies

'...even the good-natured youngster who volunteers to buy a quarter of cannabis to share with his friends and happens to get caught will be regarded by the law, the police, the school and the rest of society as a drug dealer.'

In accordance with UK government targets, all schools (primary and secondary) should by now have drug policies in place, providing details of their drugs education programmes as well as details of how they manage drug-related incidents.

In managing incidents, many schools will now automatically call in the police to deal with the situation. However, the school or the police will ensure the child's parents or guardians are also brought in (if they are 17, or 16 in Scotland, this won't be done if the young person asks for them not to be involved), but depending on the severity of the incident, e.g. taking into account the type of drug and whether or not the child intended to sell it, this need not necessarily result in an arrest or exclusion from school.

However, if a child is caught supplying drugs, this will always be regarded as a serious offence. Your child should know that even the good-natured youngster who volunteers to buy a quarter of cannabis to share with his friends and happens to get caught will be regarded by the law, the police, the school and the rest of society as a drug dealer.

What happens if your child is held for questioning by the police?

- If the child is under 17 (or 16 in Scotland), the police should notify you where and why he/she is being held, and should not question him/her without you (or in your absence, a social worker) being present.

- Your child is also entitled to have a solicitor if he or she is being questioned by the police.

- In England and Wales, the youngster can be detained for up to 24 hours (or 36 hours if the offence is serious) without any charges being made. In Scotland, the detention time limit is six hours. After that time, they should either be released, charged with an offence or a court warrant should be issued allowing him/her to be held for a further period without charge (nb: the last option is not applicable in Scotland).

Reprimands and final warnings

In England and Wales, a new reprimand and final warning scheme was introduced under the Crime and Disorder Act 1998 to replace police cautioning of young offenders.

If your child is not charged, but has committed a minor offence and is a first-time offender, a reprimand may be given by the police. Any further offending results in either a final warning or charge. The final warning triggers immediate referral to a local Youth Offending Team, which will assess the young person and, unless they consider it inappropriate, prepare a 'Change' (rehabilitation) programme aimed at preventing any future offending. Reprimands and warnings are recordable and citeable in court.

In Scotland, should any child aged eight to16 be charged with a drugs offence, a report will always be sent to the Children's Reporter who then decides on the course of action. In the case of anyone aged 16 or over, the decision on whether or not to prosecute, or to issue a caution, rests with the Procurator Fiscal.

Prosecution

If your child is arrested at the age of 17 or over (or 16 or over in Scotland), he or she could be brought to trial in a criminal court. Being found guilty of a drugs offence means a criminal record for life – a sobering thought when you consider the following implications.

A criminal record for a drugs offence could:

- Affect a young person's career prospects. Many employers are entitled to have access to a job candidate's criminal records (e.g. armed forces, emergency services, government agencies, employers with responsibilities involving children). Most employers will have plenty of choice when it comes to prospective employees – and most won't choose one with a criminal record.

- Prevent them from visiting certain countries. People with criminal records may not be granted visas for entering certain countries – a fact which could cause problems in certain jobs involving travelling, as well as curb holiday plans.
- Affect a person's ability to obtain life assurance or a mortgage.

Apart from the formal consequences, a criminal conviction can bring a lot of unwanted social baggage too. For example, the youngster and his/her family may be ostracised by the neighbourhood, which could lead to arguments, isolation and problems at school or work.

Hitting home

When discussing the issue with their youngsters, it's well worth noting that many professionals who work with drugs and young people advise parents to focus more on the social than the health implications of taking drugs (although it is still important to point out the health risks). They believe that the prospect of not being able to travel/get the job they want/buy a place of their own has far more impact than warnings about short and long-term health risks. As one senior drugs worker puts it: 'Healthwise, teenagers think they are invincible, but possible restrictions to their present or future lifestyle will make them sit up and take notice'.

Drug testing

Drug testing is becoming increasingly widespread in industry and in sport. Police forces also carry out random drug-testing on people visiting clubs and pubs as a condition of entry. Some schools, particularly private schools, have begun drug-testing their students, and kits are now available for home use. Testing can be carried out on urine, blood and hair samples, and skin swabs can also be taken. Drug testing is a highly controversial subject, with many people seeing it as an invasion of privacy. Here are some issues to bear in mind:

- The results of drug tests – especially from home testing kits – are not always accurate. There is a possibility of having false positive or false negative results.

- Many drugs can be detected by a urine test between one and four days after use. However, regular use of cannabis may make drug detection possible up to 30 days after it has last been used.

- It is important that young people are aware that applying for certain jobs may involve taking a drug test – the results of which may have a dramatic effect on their future career.

Summing Up

Potentially, a seemingly harmless experiment with a drug as commonly used as cannabis could have repercussions throughout a young person's life. For this reason, many people – including some police chiefs – believe drug possession offences (without intention to supply) should be dealt with in a different manner, perhaps through drug courts which would deal more leniently with minor offenders. This, they believe, gives problem users a chance to seek help rather than landing them with a prison sentence and criminal record. But however you choose to look at the law's attitude to drug offenders, the present penalties can seriously affect a young person's future.

We owe it to them to point out the facts about what could happen if they are caught in possession of, or supplying, drugs. If they have this information they can make their own choices. And, for some, the thought of a criminal record, or even of being in trouble with the police, will be enough of a deterrent.

Be aware and make sure your child is aware of the basic legal points outlined in this chapter.

- Let them know (in a non-threatening manner) what the penalties could be if they are caught in possession of, or supplying, illegal drugs.

- Spell out the fact that supplying drugs is always dealt with seriously – and that the person who shares out cannabis or any other drugs with friends is regarded by the law as a dealer.

- Use the real-life case studies to illustrate how being caught with drugs has seriously affected the lives of some young people. If this has happened to anyone you both know personally, why not talk through the various implications it will have/has had, e.g. on their career, travel plans, etc.

- Ask your child about his/her school's drug policy – make sure they understand what could happen if they were found with drugs in school.

Chapter Eight

Drugs in the Family

How can I tell if my child is taking drugs?

It's natural for parents to want to know how to spot the signs of drug use so they can look out for the 'danger signals' in their children. But as we saw in chapter 2, this is not necessarily a helpful approach for two main reasons:

- Signs associated with drug-taking can be mistaken for normal teenage behaviour or other problems not related to drugs.

- If your child realises what you're up to, it could betray his or her trust in you. Think about it from the young person's point of view: going through adolescence is a touchy enough business without feeling your every move is being monitored by an over-anxious parent.

That said, as a parent you are in the best position to notice if your child is upset or anxious about something. If their behaviour is causing you concern, you have every right to try to find out what is bothering them.

Some parents may be attracted to the idea of drug testing. Home-testing kits are now being advertised specifically at parents. However, any parent wishing to broach the subject with their child should think very carefully before doing so. Not only is this more than likely to be seen by the young person as an invasion of their privacy and a huge betrayal of trust, the results of these kits are also not 100% reliable and could therefore cause undue hurt and misunderstanding within a family.

Bearing all this in mind, overleaf is a list of signs which may – or may not – indicate that your child is having problems of some sort.

- Sudden changes of mood.

- Uncharacteristic aggression or irritability.

- Prolonged loss of appetite.

- Lack of interest in hobbies, friends or schoolwork.

- Unexplained loss of money or possessions (including those of other people).

- Lies and secretive behaviour.

- Prolonged bouts of tiredness or sleeplessness.

- Sores around the mouth and nose, enlargement of pupils.

- Unusual stains and smells on clothes.

'Think about it from the young person's point of view: going through adolescence is a touchy enough business without feeling your every move is being monitored by an over-anxious parent.'

If you are concerned about your child's behaviour, you may find it useful to discuss this in confidence with your partner or another family member, or even a trusted teacher or family doctor. However you may feel about involving anyone else, it is always a good idea to talk to your child and show that you are concerned rather than accusing them of anything. Try using the communication techniques outlined in chapter 6 to broach the subject.

Drug evidence

Although it's unlikely you will find actual drugs in the house (and remember it is not conducive to a trusting relationship to snoop round in your child's bedroom), you may come across the following evidence of drug taking:

- Scorched tin foil (not necessarily a sign of heroin or crack use – some people heat cannabis oil on tin foil and then inhale the fumes).

- Empty plastic bags smelling of glue.

- Burnished knives (heated knives are often used to cut cannabis resin).

If you do discover your child is taking drugs

Throughout this guide you've been advised not to panic about drugs, to approach the issue calmly and to find out the facts. Understandably, that's not easy to do. Being calm and non-judgmental about such an emotive subject flies in the face of many people's instincts. It's hard for parents to be objective about something they regard as a dangerous threat to their children. And it's doubly hard if they discover their children are actually experimenting with that threat.

Parents who find out that their children are taking drugs often experience a maelstrom of conflicting emotions: they may feel angry, disgusted, frightened, disappointed, bewildered, grief-stricken, hurt and depressed – all at the same time. The last thing they feel is calm, open-minded and ready to understand. But difficult as they may be to adopt, these attitudes are essential.

In the last chapter, we saw how staying open-minded about what a person is telling us can help us to understand them better. Understanding a person's feelings and actions can help us to help them understand themselves and why they are behaving in a certain way. They may also see how their behaviour is affecting the people they care for. There are no guarantees, but if they reach this stage, and know they have our support, they have a better chance of dealing with their problem behaviour.

We also saw that jumping to conclusions, preaching and laying down the law are natural reactions, but do nothing to help take the understanding process forward. Threats about calling the police or throwing them out of the house will destroy their trust in you and may make the situation far worse.

If your child is taking drugs and knows you have found out, he or she will need your understanding and support. You can give them that if you bear in mind everything we've learned so far.

'…jumping to conclusions, preaching and laying down the law are natural reactions, but do nothing to help take the understanding process forward.'

Remember

- You now know the facts about drugs. This will keep the hype-induced horrors at bay.

- You also know there are various reasons why young people take drugs and you can use this to help you understand why your own child is using them.

- What's more, you've picked up some practical tips on good communication, which will not only help you broach this difficult subject with better self-control, but will also help you and your child to keep talking.

There is no magic formula that will sort everything out if you and your child find yourselves in this particular situation. Every family has different ways of dealing with difficult issues. As we saw in chapter 4, the reasons behind the drug-taking may vary enormously and perhaps require different responses, depending on how regularly it occurs and whether there are any underlying problems triggering it off.

However, these general guidelines may help you cope with the situation in a rational way, which can only be of benefit to your child, yourself and the rest of your family.

'The reasons behind the drug-taking may vary enormously and perhaps require different responses, depending on how regularly it occurs and whether there are any underlying problems triggering it off.'

Coping strategy

- Don't panic.

- Don't jump to conclusions that your child is a regular drug user.

- Don't fly off the handle. No matter how upset you are, try to stay calm in front of your child.

- Start talking. Tell them you know they have been using drugs and try to find out more. But remember, no Spanish Inquisition tactics – a sympathetic attitude will be far more helpful.

- Really listen to what they say to you. Look out for signs of hostility, fear, sheepishness or anxiety – these will give you an indication of whether the drug-taking was simply an experiment, done just for fun or whether there may be underlying reasons such as unhappiness or pressure. Tell them what you think they are feeling in a non-judgmental way (see 'active listening' section in chapter 6). Realising that you are not going to create a scene and that you want to listen to them may encourage them to open up to you.

▪ Use your knowledge about drugs to discuss some of the important issues.

▪ A useful exercise, particularly with younger teenagers, is to give them some paper and ask them to write down in separate lists the positive and the negative aspects associated with taking drugs. Doing this helps them to think things through for themselves, which they may not have done before. This technique is used very successfully by one particular Scottish youth drugs programme, whose manager reports that the young person's negatives list is almost always longer than the positives list. This provides a powerful learning experience (it has come from the youngster himself/herself) and a good starting point for a meaningful discussion.

▪ Be realistic. Talking with your child will help reinforce your trust in each other and will show them that they have your support. But it won't necessarily end the drug-taking.

▪ Seek the support you need. Trying to cope in this situation is emotionally very taxing. No matter how calmly you have behaved in front of your child, inside you will probably still be experiencing all the natural feelings of anger, worry, etc. You may also have dozens of questions about what has happened, but not necessarily wish to talk to anyone who knows you or your child. The good news is there's no need to cope on your own. There are many people who can help you, no matter what your concern about drugs may be.

'Be realistic. Talking with your child will help reinforce your trust in each other and will show them that they have your support. But it won't necessarily end the drug-taking.'

Support is always at hand

There are several kinds of support available to you and your child. The choice may vary depending on where in the UK you live and whether you live in a rural or urban community, but what is important is that support in some form or another is there if you need it. Here is a brief summary of the levels of support available. Contact details can be found in the help list.

Local professionals

Your own GP or local social work department will be able to advise you about the availability of services in your area.

Drug information websites

There is a wealth of drug information and advice available on the Internet. A list of useful and reliable sites can be found in the help list section.

National drug helplines

These also are listed in the help list section at the back of this book. They provide confidential information and advice on all aspects of drugs and drug use, as well as information about legal matters and local services available to you.

Specialist drug services

These provide confidential information and advice on drugs and drugs-related issues (i.e. treatment centres, legal and housing issues) for drug users and their families, either by phone or face-to-face (some may use an appointment system; others may operate on a drop-in basis). They may also provide a counselling service.

Support services specifically for families of drug users

Among the services available to families are information websites, 24-hour helplines, one-to-one counselling, visits from drug workers, workshops and local support groups.

Hospital clinics

Hospital out-patient clinics throughout the UK provide treatment for drug dependence (mainly heroin), which may include a methadone programme to help users come off heroin and social work/psychological counselling support. The services provided differ from hospital to hospital, but most clinics are not generally in a position to provide help with other drug problems.

Residential services

These are generally for people with serious, long-term drug problems.

Summing Up

Coping with the knowledge that your child is taking drugs may be one of the most difficult challenges you may face as a parent. As with many other issues which confront families from time to time, it will require patience and a calm and sensitive approach.

If you can talk to your child about what is happening in an honest and non-judgmental manner, you have a better chance of facing up to any potential problems together as trusting friends rather than adversaries.

It may come to light that the truth about your child's drug-taking is not as earth-shattering as you had at first thought. Alternatively, you may unearth a deeper problem which requires professional support.

Whatever may happen, neither you, your child, nor anyone else in the family need ever feel alone. Never be afraid to ask for help. Whether it's basic information about drugs, someone to talk to in confidence, advice or medical assistance, there are resources and people out there that can give you the support you need.

- Be aware of the signs of possible drug use – but bear in mind they could also be part of normal growing up or indicate another problem.

- Resist the temptation to hunt for evidence of drug-taking in your child's room – it could spoil a trusting relationship.

- If you do discover your child is taking drugs, use the coping strategy outlined in this chapter.

- Never be afraid to ask for help – there are plenty of people who can give you the support you need.

'Coping with the knowledge that your child is taking drugs may be one of the most difficult challenges you may face as a parent. As with many other issues which confront families from time to time, it will require patience and a calm and sensitive approach.'

Help List

Addaction

67-69 Cowcross Street, London, EC1M 6PU
Tel: 020 7251 5860
info@addaction.org.uk
www.addaction.org.uk
Drug services targeting children, young people, parents and 'hard to reach' communities.

Adfam

25 Corsham Street, London, N1 6DR
Tel: 020 7553 7640
www.adfam.org.uk
Community offering information and support to families of those with drug and alcohol problems.

Alcohol Concern

64 Leman Street, London, E1 8EU
Tel: 020 7264 0510
contact@alcoholconcern.org.uk
www.alcoholconcern.org.uk
Alcohol misuse agency working to reduce the incidence and cost of alcohol related harm. Provides information on support services.

Alcohol Focus Scotland

2nd Floor, 166 Buchanan Street, Glasgow, G1 2LW
Tel: 0141 572 6700
enquiries@alcohol-focus-scotland.org.uk
www.alcohol-focus-scotland.org.uk
The only Scottish charity working to raise awareness of the misuse of alcohol and the significant health and social consequences linked to its abuse.

ASH

First Floor, 144-145 Shoreditch High Street, London, E1 6JE
Tel: 020 7739 5902
enquiries@ash.co.uk
www.ash.org.uk
Charity aimed at achieving eventual elimination of the health problems caused by tobacco.

British Red Cross

44 Moorfields, London, EC2Y 9AL
Tel: 0844 871 11 11
information@redcross.org.uk
www.redcross.org.uk
First aid training. A range of other first aid training agencies can also be found in Yellow Pages or on the Internet.

Centre for Recovery

Tel: 01970 626470
www.recovery.org.uk
UK information and advice centre for drug and alcohol abuse.

Crew 2000

32 Cockburn Street, Edinburgh, EH1 1PB
Tel: 0131 220 3404
admin@crew2000.org.uk
www.crew2000.co.uk
Website produced by a group of young people, providing information on how to reduce the risks involved in using drugs.

Dads Against Drugs

48 Kirklands Road, Hull, HU5 5AU
Tel: 01482 228881
Drugs hotline: 0800 138 0941
info@dadsagainstdrugs.karoo.co.uk
www.dadsagainstdrugs.co.uk
Promoting anti-drug messages through football, theatre, community projects
and schools.

Drinkline

Tel: 0800 917 8282
Confidential advice and information on drinking.

Drugs Education Forum

c/o Mentor UK, 4th Floor, 74 Great Eastern Street, London, EC2A 3JG
Tel: 020 739 8494
def@mentoruk.org
www.drugseducation.org.uk
Works to provide effective drugs education for all young people in England.

drugs.gov.uk

Direct Communications Unit, 2 Marsham Street, London, SW1P 4DF
Tel: 0207 035 4848
www.drugs.homeoffice.gov.uk
public.enquiries@homeoffice.gsi.gov.uk
Cross-government national drug strategy website for drug prevention and
treatment professionals, and others interested in the drug strategy. Also
provides details of local DATs.

Drugscope

Prince Consort House, Suite 204 (2nd Floor), 109/111 Farringdon Road, London, EC1R 3BW
Tel: 0207 520 7550
info@drugscope.org.uk
www.drugscope.org.uk
Charity aiming to inform policy development and reduce drug-related risk.

Drugworld

www.drugworld.co.uk
A website that provides drugs information for young people.

Families Anonymous

Doddington & Rollo Community Association, Charlotte Despard Avenue, Battersea, London, SW11 5HD
Tel: 0845 1200 660
office@famanon.org.uk
www.famanon.org.uk
Self-help organisation made up of friends and family of those involved in drug abuse. Provides support and advice for users and relatives.

Familyrapp.com

PO Box 117, Oxted, RH8 0FN
Tel: 01883 723710
info@familyrapp.com
www.familyrapp.com
Family-based website including drugs information for parents.

Fast Forward

4 Bernard Street, Edinburgh, EH6 6PP
Tel: 0131 554 4300
admin@fastforward.org.uk
www.fastforward.org.uk
Voluntary organisation which promotes health through education by focusing on the prevention of drug, alcohol and tobacco misuse.

FRANK

Tel: 0800 77 66 00
frank@talktofrank.com
www.talktofrank.com
National (England & Wales) drugs information and advice campaign.

Health Development Agency (England) (Now NICE)

www.nice.org.uk
As a result of the Department of Health's 2004 review of its 'arms length bodies', the functions of the HDA were transferred to NICE.

Health Education Board for Scotland

Tel: 0131 536 5500
general_enquiries@health.scot.nhs.uk
www.healthscotland.com/drugs.aspx
Provides links to organisations dealing with drug misuse.

Health Promotion Agency for Northern Ireland

18 Ormeau Avenue, Belfast, BT2 8HS
Tel: 028 9031 1611
info@hpani.org.uk
www.healthpromotionagency.org.uk
Works to prioritise health in all areas of society.

Health Promotion Division, National Assembly of Wales

Tel: 029 2068 1239
hplibrary@wales.gsi.gov.uk
www.hpw.wales.gov.uk
Provides information on health promotion and health professional issues.

Healthy Schools

www.healthyschools.gov.uk
Health information for teachers and pupils at Key Stages 1-4.

HIT

3 Paramount Business Park, Wilson Road, Liverpool, L36 6AW
Tel: 0844 412 0973
stuff@hit.org.uk
www.hit.org.uk
Effective interventions on drugs, community safety and other public health concerns.

Know Cannabis

www.knowcannabis.org.uk
Support for cutting down or stopping use of cannabis.

Know the Score (NHS Health Scotland)

Tel: 0800 587 587 9
www.knowthescore.info
Information and advice on drugs in Scotland for parents, children and professionals.

Lifeline

101-103 Oldham Street, Manchester, M4 1LW
Tel: 0161 834 7160
webeditor@lifeline.org.uk
www.lifelineproject.co.uk
Helps people who use drugs and the families of those who use drugs.

Narcotics Anonymous

202 City Road, London, EC1V 2PH
Tel: 0845 373 3366 or 020 7730 0009
nahelpline@ukna.org
www.ukna.org
Self-help group network.

NHS Health Scotland

Tel: 0131 536 5500
www.healthscotland.com
Provides information on a range of topics, including alcohol and drugs.

Over-Count Drugs Information and Advice Agency

Tel: 01387 770404 (every Tues evening, 7-10pm)
info@over-count.org.uk
www.over-count.org.uk
Provides advice on all aspects concerning the misuse of any over-the-counter, non-prescription drug.

PADA (Parents Against Drug Abuse)

Tel: 0845 702 3867 (helpline)
admin@pada.org.uk
www.pada.org.uk
National organisation that provides support to families of substance users.

Release

388 Old Street, London, EC1V 9LT
Tel: 0845 4500 215 (drugs helpline)
ask@release.org.uk
www.release.org.uk
Specialist services for professionals and the public concerning drugs and the law.

Re-Solv

30a High Street, Stone, Staffordshire, ST15 8AW
Tel: 01785 810 762
information@re-solv.org
www.re-solv.org
UK charity dedicated to the prevention of solvent and volatile substance abuse.

RIDE Foundation

The Mansion, Claremont Drive, Esher, Surrey, KT10 9LY
Tel: 01372 467708
info@ridefoundation.org.uk
www.ridefoundation.org.uk
Charity dedicated to the promotion of life skills and drug education in schools.

Scottish Drugs Forum (SDF)

91 Mitchell Street, Glasgow, G1 3LN
Tel: 0141 221 1175
enquiries@sdf.org.uk
www.sdf.org.uk
National non-government drugs policy and information agency.

TheSite.org

YouthNet UK, First Floor, 50 Featherstone Street, London, EC1Y 8RT
Tel: 0207 250 5700
www.thesite.org/info/drugs
Online youth advice and information service.

Turning Point

Standon House, 21 Mansell Street, London, E1 8AA
Tel: 0207 481 7600
info@turning-point.co.uk
www.turning-point.co.uk
Works in partnership with local and national services (England & Wales) to help people with problems relating to drink, drugs, mental health and learning difficulties.

Urban75

www.urban75.com/Drugs/index.html
Online drugs resource that neither condemns nor condones drug use.

Wired Initiative

enquiries@wiredinitiative.com

www.wiredinitiative.com
Online portal raising awareness and understanding of substance misuse, the problems it creates and the ways to deal with these problems.

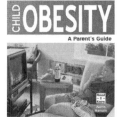
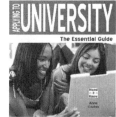
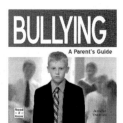